RELATIONSHIP BASED LEADERSHIP

DISCARD

Kathleen Earle

University Press of America,® Inc.
Lanham · Boulder · New York · Toronto · Oxford

Contents

Preface

Many directors of early childhood programs have little training in program management. Some start as teachers or aides, learning as they go. Even those with college degrees seldom begin with appropriate management training. As a result, many fall back on management techniques observed along the way. Unfortunately, these techniques may be poorly suited for managing teams of professionals in early childhood programs. As a result, many administrators find themselves in situations similar to that of individuals who resent their own harsh parents, but then find themselves making the same mistakes. Thus, well-motivated administrators may increasingly fall back on boss-style management, either because they know no other way or because they are desperate to "get things under control."

This old "carrot-and-stick" approach emphasizes top-down bureaucratic control and centralized planning. In the past, this form has worked pretty well in the military where control was essential, or in factories where sticking to a routine form of production got the job done. In such organizations, workers were lucky if they had managers who treated them with paternalistic kindness.

But paternalism, which emphasizes control and a "father knows best" approach, is poorly suited for non-routine work where each person is different and where motivation must come from within the worker. Childcare agencies, by their very nature, require workers who want to do more than just please the boss or treat children as routine cases.

This will not happen by admonishing top-down management to be kinder to workers. Rather, managers and workers must discover a new form of managing child-care agencies—one that emphasizes cooperation rather than control; motivation from within rather than from without; and accountability to a team, more than to a boss. Such changes not only require fundamental shifts in how managers and workers think, but even greater changes in their relationships to one another.

The Solution

How we accomplish that task is profoundly important. It won't be accomplished by a weekend workshop. Neither will it be achieved by training a few who will, in turn, train fellow workers. We need basic changes in the collective "mind-set" and fundamental shifts in how organizations are structured. It is an arduous task that may take months, or even years.

Such an investment, however, will generally be richly rewarded. Workers who see problems will work together to solve them rather than waiting for the boss to tell them what to do. Absenteeism and turnover will be reduced because workers do not want to let each other down. Stress and burnout will be reduced because workers continually see themselves as part of a great cause and because they sense the support of team members. There will still be conflict because early childhood workers will have increasingly strong feelings about what they do. But, they will experience greater support from fellow workers in effectively dealing with conflict, even to the point that strong feelings become a source of innovation and group solidarity.

Fortunately, the pioneering work needed to create such agencies has been underway for over fifty years. Initiated by social psychologists in lab experiments, it then grew as "quality circles" in large corporations. In countries like Japan, Germany, and the United States, it has become the management philosophy by which entire markets have been captured. Companies that hold onto the old control model lose market share to those that empower their workers and to those that see the customer's satisfaction as everyone's task.

In education, some schools have adopted similar principles in what has become known as "the Quality Movement." Not only do teachers and administrators work in a team environment, but students are also empowered and treated as team members in the classroom. Students take responsibility for much of their own education, using teachers more as resources than as dispensers of knowledge. Likewise, students are internally motivated to seek knowledge rather than just data and information because it might be on an exam.

It is important, of course, to ask whether a form of management pioneered in industry and still under development in education can work in early childhood agencies. After all, children are not products, and very young children can't be expected to make adult decisions. Our position is that early childhood programs enjoy certain advantages over industries and schools. Interaction among caregivers in early childcare centers is, by its very nature, more team-like than that of public school teachers or production workers. In addition, workers in early childcare programs can enjoy a much greater sense of "cause" or "mission" than production workers. Making better widgets doesn't hold a candle to nurturing a new human life.

The last few years have seen a great increase in publicly-funded early childcare programs. Early Head Start programs have an especially recent history. As these programs continue to grow, we have a window of opportunity to insure that new forms of management become institutionalized. We also have the rare opportunity of helping program leaders implement models of leadership that bring out the best in workers and promote a cooperative team spirit.

Features

- **Strong Research Base.** Most of the principles and practices described have been tested using control groups and before-after comparisons. In addition, the research is based on studies measuring changes in behavior and performance, rather than attitude surveys that ask participants to rate how much they liked some program or activity.
- **Principles over Practices.** Though the book teaches certain skills and management practices, its primary focus is on principles of leadership. A principle consists of basic truths that orient behavior in a many diverse situations. Principles, when internalized, provide leaders with answers in a wide variety of situations, while techniques are much more specific to particular situations.
- **Applied Focus.** The book employs case studies, many of which were obtained by means of extensive on-site interviews with program directors. In addition, a variety of learning exercises allows learners to apply the principles and skills presented in each chapter.
- **Tailored to Early Childhood Programs.** The case studies and anecdotal examples are derived primarily from experiences in actual early childcare settings. Rather than a book about business adapted to childcare programs, the book is focused on applying universal leadership principles in childcare situations.
- **Clearly Written.** Jargon and academic language are kept to a minimum. The level of writing should be clearly understood by childcare leaders with even the most basic educational backgrounds.
- **Field Tested.** Preliminary drafts of the manuscript have been field tested in: a) a doctoral seminar in educational leadership at the University of Texas-Pan American; b) an early childhood management senior-level course at Texas Tech University; and c) select early childhood programs in the Southwestern United States.

Chapter 1.
"The Times, They are A'Changing."
Leadership in the Twenty-first Century

Chapter Summary

This chapter emphasizes the need to make a shift from bureaucratic or "control" models of management to team leadership. It proposes that ordinary managers can learn to apply basic principles and develop the essential skills of team leadership. This shift requires fundamental changes in the structure of early childhood programs and a reformulation of the collective mindset or the organizational culture.

Introduction

Martha is a dedicated teacher. She cares deeply about the children in her program and has a strong commitment to the principles of early childhood intervention. Nevertheless, when asked how she feels about her work, she reports, "I love the work, but I hate the job."

She loves the children and has an excellent relationship with many of the moms who drop them off every day. "They are not the problem," she says. "It's all the rules and the red tape. My director seems to care more about procedures and looking good for our next inspection than she does about how the children are progressing. She used to be a teacher—one of the best. I don't know what happened to her when they made her director. All of a sudden, she starts making rules and treating us like children. We used to have a lot of cooperation among the teachers. When the toddlers' teachers had some time, they would come over to our side and help with the babies. We'd do the same with them when we had the babies asleep. Now, we're told to stick to assigned duties, and we've lost a lot of the team spirit we used to feel.

To make matters worse, some of the teachers spend a lot of time complaining about the parents and the community. Sure, they've got problems, but I think they're doing pretty well, considering the poverty and the uncertainty they have to live with. They may have a lot to learn about what it means to be a parent, but that is what we're supposed to be here for.

She says she wants us to come to her with our problems, but she's not very approachable. One of the teachers tried to tell her how we felt, but ___ (the director) got real defensive and refused to admit that she had a problem. As much as I would miss the babies, I'm thinking about finding a job somewhere else. They don't pay enough for me to put up with this kind of treatment."[1]

These days, it's tough directing a program like Early Head Start. Some directors come to their positions with minimal training in administration. They have to please state and federal agencies, motivate child care professional, manage budgets, get more parental involvement, fight off interference, settle disputes, and otherwise keep a lot of people happy. Many of them also love the work their agencies do, but have a difficult time with their jobs.

This book is written to provide help for directors and their child care professionals. One does not need a degree in management to be a good director. Neither does one have to be a charismatic leader to be effective. Much can be done by ordinary people who learn to apply some key principles and develop a few essential skills. Management of early childhood programs can be as pleasant and rewarding as the work of caring for needy children.

Bureaucracy as a Problem

Let's start with a few of the basics. Initially, we need to show that many of the problems commonly assumed to be the result of personality conflicts are, in reality, the consequence of how an organization is structured—or the way relationships are arranged and bureaucratically organized. Everyone likes to curse bureaucracy, but few realize it is a vast improvement over the type of organization that preceded it. We will show how some aspects of bureaucracy are counterproductive in child care programs, then describe some relatively new forms of organizational structure that work much better.

Several examples will help us illustrate how organizational structure can be as important as having the right personality.

Several years ago, a large hospital was having problems with its receiving clerk, the person responsible for keeping up inventory and getting needed supplies for all the different departments. In essence, the man was crotchety, curt, and often rude. The hospital director was tired of hearing worker complaints about the man, so he decided to replace him. He asked the personnel director to look for someone who had a reputation for getting along with others and treating people well. After a careful search, they found just such a person. Following the change, everything went well for a time. Then, the new person started acting just like the previous clerk. Directors again started complaining about delays and rude comments.

An organizational consultant, who happened to be working on another problem, was asked to look at the situation with the new receiving clerk. The director was surprised with his analysis. "It's not surprising that you're having this problem," he said. "You have the position structured so that everyone in the hospital can give orders and complain to your receiving clerk. No wonder you get a grouch. Such conditions would wear anyone down." According to the recommendation of the consultant, the clerk was put under the supervision of a department head. Those who had complaints directed them to this individual. Amazingly, the new clerk soon had back his sunny disposition.

A similar lesson was learned a number of years ago in restaurants. It was not uncommon to find a lot of conflict between the cooks (who were mostly men) and the wait staff (who were mostly women). Waitresses would complain about cooks always getting their orders wrong and about them being slow or abrupt. The cooks also complained about how bossy the waitresses could get, and how they would constantly harass the cooks about getting their orders out.

A sociologist who studied the situation pinpointed the problem. While the status and pay of the cooks was supposed to be higher than the wait staff, they saw themselves as having to take orders from and being hassled by individuals with a supposedly lower rank. The problems were solved with a relatively simple device that you've probably seen in many restaurants—a rotating order wheel. The wait staff place orders on the wheel from which the cooks can take information without appearing to be taking "orders." This simple device changes the nature of the structured relationship and is effective in resolving a "personality problem."

Similar situations occur in early childhood programs. Directors often try to set up their organizations in the same way they have seen it done in other settings. The director in the opening story, for example, instituted many rules and policies because that was how she had always seen other agencies run. Because she also believed that everyone should have his or her own job and stick to it, she also set up rather rigid job divisions. Finally, since she believed that a boss should maintain a certain distance from subordinates in order to be impartial, she made herself less accessible. All these structural changes vastly affected her relations with co-workers and contributed to the problems described by the teacher.

It would be erroneous to conclude that bureaucracy is to blame for all mismanagement and organizational dysfunctions. As we indicated earlier, bureaucracy is a great improvement over the type of organization that preceded it. Though these earlier organizations could be called a lot of things, the term "cronyism" is quite descriptive. The following case study, conducted in the 1950's by sociologist Alvin Gouldner, is a good example of this type of organization.

A small-town gypsum plant had undergone a dramatic change. For many years, the plant had been a comfortable part of the local community. The personnel department hired only local residents because of the belief that city people could not be trusted. Staff members who came in late, drunk, or not at all, were seldom disciplined, and few people were ever fired. The basic rationale for this treatment of employees was, "You can't ride the men very hard when they're your neighbors."

The plant was loved by the staff and the local community. Local farmers, as well as child care professionals, brought equipment to be fixed for free in the shop. Each employee could usually work where he or she felt most accepted and comfortable. The company made promotions on the basis of friendship or prestige in the community. Staff members seldom tried to figure out better ways to do their jobs. They simply did the work the way it had always been done.

While the staff members were happy, the plant was very unproductive. Eventually, its central management, located in a distant city, could no longer justify poor productivity. When "Old Doug," the plant manager died, the firm sent in a new man who was told to make the plant more efficient. He immediately began to bureaucratize the plant, demoting or firing inefficient staff members. In addition, he hired or promoted replacements on the basis of what they knew rather than whom they knew. He insisted on accurate records and made people work in the specialization for which they were hired. He made and enforced rules against using company property for personal use. The staff and the town were very unhappy with the changes. But in spite of a wildcat strike, over time the plant became more efficient and profitable.[2]

As this example illustrates, bureaucracy can be frustrating, but it is an improvement over cronyism, the older autocratic form of management that preceded it. There are still a few autocratic early childhood agencies around. In one or two with which we are familiar, cronyism is common with poorly skilled friends of the boss appointed to key positions. Leaders in these autocratic organizations often use the resources and power of their agencies to "feather their nests," or abuse the power of their positions to gain personal privilege. In such organizations, loyalty to the boss is more important than providing quality child care. Rules are often less important than determining the whims of arbitrary bosses. While these may be enjoyable places to work for the privileged few, other child care professionals tend to live in fear of not pleasing these autocratic top leaders. Most notably, quality child care seldom happens.

In a bureaucracy, rules and top-down control keep people from "feathering their nests," or from using organizational resources for personal benefit. These organizations move away from arbitrary whims toward rules calculated to produce the greatest benefits for the organization. In bureaucratic organizations, everyone is responsible to a boss who has gained his or her position through merit. These bosses are given authority to enforce rules designed to protect the interests of the organization.

Still, bureaucratic organizations often have problems of their own. Often, for example, rules that originally made sense become outdated as situations change. Bureaucracy is often poorly suited to organizations that must deal with many different individual needs. That rigidity is illustrated in the following case study of a juvenile treatment center.

> Our agency had a rule that the parents could come and visit the children every other Sunday. I remember feeling frustrated over this, as I felt that it was hardly enough contact. I remember asking how this decision was arrived at and being told by my supervisor that he didn't know: it had always been that way. I always felt that the bureaucratic process placed a great gap between the social child care professional and the client. This created much frustration because, I guess, I felt some human feelings toward these people and couldn't give them what I wanted to. There were too many regulations and forms that got in the way of what I considered to be a good relationship based on needs and feelings. Thus, I didn't last long.[3]

Rules can also get in the way of effective action in early childhood agencies. In one agency, for example, a rule was announced restricting child care professional from bringing their own children to the monthly evening parent meetings at the Center. Top management thought the child care professional were abusing this privilege to get free babysitting for their own children. Many teachers, however, were not abusing the opportunity. One teacher, for example, brought her teenage daughter to watch the older children so that her mother and the other teachers could help the parents interact with their little ones. This teacher had not even asked for pay for the babysitting. The new rule disrupted a valuable service provided by a committed teacher. This teacher stated, "Now, we have to pay someone, and I cannot attend because I cannot leave my daughter home alone at night. It was working so well before. I wish they would have just left it alone."

Hiring and promotion decisions in a bureaucracy are made on the basis of merit rather than on friendships and family ties that were most important in autocratic organizations. Bureaucratic philosophy holds that what you know should be given much greater importance than who you know. Bureaucracies rely on highly specialized job descriptions to ensure that work can be coordinated and that each person is responsible for only a small portion of a much larger process. This makes it possible for people to be well trained in their own areas, but uninformed about what everyone else is doing.

Bureaucratic structure works well when work is highly routinized or when tight control is needed. The gypsum factory, for example, was designed to yield the same product year after year. Work there was highly routine, so bureaucracy made it more efficient. Each child care professional could be given a task that was repeated day after day, and he or she could become good at it. Military organizations are also well served by bureaucratic organization because they require strict obedience to command. An army can't have soldiers questioning every command. Military organizations that have highly bureaucratic structures can be very powerful (as the German Army proved in World War II).

But child care is neither highly routine nor can it be greatly regimented. No two children are alike, so a factory-like approach is doomed to failure. Indeed, if child care staff are professionals, they should be able to respond to the differences in children with decisions based on sound judgment and a strong commitment to high quality care. If you don't have child care professionals with good judgment and strong internal commitment, your organization is in trouble. You will have to make every decision and constantly monitor them. You, your staff, and the children will suffer. As we pointed out earlier, however, child care professionals are generally products of the types of organizations in which they work. Many child care professionals find it difficult to maintain strong commitments to children in a highly bureaucratized agency, as the following case illustrates.

> For a long time, I felt my role with the bureaucracy was to deal with human needs. In recent years, they have been stressing accountability, so I spend a lot of time completing forms and compiling records. In many instances, my work is duplicated by others, and there is less and less time that I can devote to rendering service to the children. My director is really caught up in this control situation and is constantly seeking new control methods. Now, we have new sign-in and sign-out procedures, a daily log, and weekly, bi-weekly, monthly, and yearly reports. Recently, we had to start a new management information retrieval system. Now, they analyze the data to try to control everything we do. Before all this paperwork, there was more productivity. It seems like accountability and productivity are not compatible.[4]

Team Leadership

Fortunately, you have another alternative to the regimentation of bureaucracy or the chaos of autocratic organizations. This new form goes by many names; however, "team management" is probably the most common (though we prefer the term "Team Leadership). Don't be fooled by the label. A lot of bosses claim to have instituted team leadership in their organizations when a closer examination shows they have not. A typical statement from someone in such a situation might be similar to the following account.

> Our director is always talking about teamwork and supporting the team. To her, though, teamwork means "Do what I say, without any questions." She seems to think that supporting the team means supporting her. In her mind, a team is a group of people who mindlessly follows orders. That may work for Little League, but it doesn't work for a group of highly committed child care specialists.

Team management is about much more than being "team players" or having "team spirit." When done correctly, it produces child care professionals who feel a strong sense of ownership for the quality of care provided and a deep commitment to excellent results and good relationships. It also spreads this commitment to parents and to the community served by your agency. Everyone becomes a stakeholder and shares responsibility for making things work well.

Such benefits do not come easily, however. Directors will have to share control with people who may not be as expert as they are. It also takes time and patience. Many decisions will take longer. You will have to take risks in trusting people who may not be completely ready for more responsibility. You will have to learn to motivate people with something besides the old "carrot-and-stick" approach. Even so, benefits to yourself, your child care professionals, and especially to the children entrusted to your care will be magnificent. It is worth all the effort and frustration necessary to build such an organization.

Before we explain further the nature of team leaderships, let's make a brief comparison of it with the two other types of organizations we have discussed. This comparison is made in the following figure.

The type of organization you promote will have a lot to do with the type of leader you want to become. Bureaucratic organizations tend to attract or produce *transactional* leaders, or leaders who handle the transactions needed to make an organization run smoothly. *Transactional* leaders use the authority of their positions to reward high performers or to reprimand and punish those who do not keep up with numerical expectations.[5]

Organizations that stress team leadership, on the other hand, tend to attract and produce *transformational* leaders. These are people who are more interested in helping the people they work with to transform themselves. They help their people grasp the importance of their work. One of the authors had an experience that illustrates both types of leadership.

> It was great working for my first director. She gave me freedom to do whatever I felt was necessary to make the program successful. After working for her for several years, she called me in to see what plans I had for my future. She said she couldn't see me doing the same thing a few years down the road. She encouraged me to go to graduate

school, something I never thought I would do. Then, she moved on with her career, and I got a new boss. This woman had definite ideas of what I could and could not do. I could not leave the Center unless I notified her, and I had to call her when I returned. She gave me tasks to do, and I was doing only those things she had assigned. She only seemed interested in things running smoothly, and I felt no concern whatever from her about my development or well being.

As this example illustrates, transformational leaders are always looking for ways to help their people grow personally while accomplishing organizational purposes. In this respect, transformational leaders are

Figure 1.1

Comparison of Three Types Of Organizational Leadership

	Autocratic	Bureaucratic	Team Leadership
How the Leader Uses Power	Rewards loyalty, punishes enemies & uses power for personal gain.	Top-down power to control & coordinate work for the organization.	Leaders use influence and share power with workers.
How Decisions Are Made and Carried Out	On the whim of the leader.	Most decisions made by formal rules & procedures	Teams jointly use principles to make & carry out decisions.
Motivation of Workers	To please or avoid angering the leader.	To follow orders with little thought or commitment.	Sense of accomplishment, team spirit, and ownership for results.
Common Effects on Work and Workers	Organizational needs are less important than leader's wishes	Can be efficient but often not effective. Work is boring—low commitment	Generally highly effective, with high morale and worker commitment.

more like gardeners who nurture people in order to accomplish important tasks. Transactional leaders, by comparison, are more like mechanics who want to fix things to make them run smoothly.

Perhaps this helps explain why bureaucratic organizations (and the pre-bureaucratic form of autocratic leadership) are poorly suited to build effective child care organizations. As you may recall, the structure of an organization has a lot to do with how child care professionals behave. Autocratic organizations, especially those that emphasize cronyism, seldom accomplish their basic purposes. Everyone is too busy trying to please the boss. Though bureaucracies can overcome this problem, they also have severe limitations. The most important of those is their great difficulty in motivating child care professionals. Let's examine two reasons why this is so.

First, while bureaucracies work well as instruments of control for organizations like the military, they rob staff in education and social welfare agencies of ownership and responsibility. If you have to do just as your boss says, then he or she also takes away your responsibility to identify needs and find solutions. In effect, you check your mind at the door and do whatever you are told.

Bureaucratic organizations maintain many ways to control your behavior. Your boss is given authority to reward or punish that behavior. He or she can require you to follow procedures and submit reports to see how well you follow these procedures. However, when someone else has that much control, many of us will do only as much as we have to, but not much more. When the boss believes that child care professionals can't be trusted, most will adopt a "what's in it for me" approach in which they expend only as much effort as they must, while trying to get as many benefits as they can in return. If things aren't going well, it's not their problem. They'll wait for the boss to solve even simple difficulties because the message they're getting is that they must turn all decisions over to the boss. Granted, many child care professionals will do more out of a sense of commitment. But gradually, that sense of commitment diminishes as individuals become cogs in the machinery of the bureaucratic organization.

The second reason bureaucracies are poor motivators is that they break work down into many tiny fragments—like tiny puzzle pieces. If you are only responsible for a small part of the overall work of the organization, you may start thinking that what you do is what matters most. You may fail to see the linkages between your job and the overall purpose of the organization. A librarian whose job is to keep the library from losing books, for example, will start seeing this function as the most important function of the library. He or she will track down books and zealously fine late returns. This may, in turn, weaken the overall mission of the library—to get books out to be read and enjoyed.

The same thing happens at a higher level. A division director in a bureaucratic organization will tend to focus exclusively on her own division's mission. Since she will be judged by how well her division does in relation to others, she will be tempted to hoard resources that are needed in other divisions, again to the detriment of the whole organization. This process, called "goal displacement," is common in bureaucratic organizations. Each person becomes so involved in tending his own area that he loses sight of linkages to the larger purposes of the organization. In many cases, he begins competing with others in ways that are counter to the mission of the company or organization. We often see this situation in hotels. A few years ago, one of the authors went to a five-star hotel in Spain at the invitation of a major university there.

> Everything was very nice until I got to my room and found that the hook for the shower head (at the end of a flexible hose) was broken and could not be used without holding it in one hand while trying to shower with the other. That's pretty hard to do and still use soap and shampoo. I left a note the next morning, but when I returned, nothing had been done. Apparently, it was not the job of the cleaning crew to fix the shower. So I called the desk and talked to the receptionist. The next day, it still was not fixed. Apparently, she

was only responsible for registering guests, so it wasn't her job either. I guessed that she had put in a call to the repair crew, but saw no need to follow up. At the end of three days, the shower still had not been fixed. Each person did his or her job but failed to pursue the overall satisfaction of their guests as the chief concern. My stay at this hotel was memorable, more because of the broken shower than for otherwise fine accommodations.

It's often easy to believe that such poor service is the result of personality flaws. We blame "lazy" or "incompetent" workers, but people respond to the structure of the organizations in which they work. When their work is limited to a small part of the overall operation, it is difficult to keep the central purpose of the organization clearly in mind. Each person does her job but fails to ensure that her own work fits together with the work done by others in service to the children. This is illustrated in the following account by one mother.

When I first enrolled my baby, I gave some lady who I met at a meeting all the information she said she needed to get me into the program. Then, another lady came by my house and asked me the same questions and made me sign a bunch of papers. Then, when I took my daughter to the Center for her first day of school, the teacher didn't know her name, age, or any of the health information I had given to the other two ladies. I wound up being late for work that day because I didn't want to leave my baby with a stranger who knew nothing about her. I was very angry with the whole place. I started to wonder if anyone there talked to anyone else and would my baby be O.K.

The uncoordinated effort of this program often results from bureaucratization. Each person becomes concentrated on her own job and fails to tie what she does to the overall mission of the agency. Goal displacement is very common in bureaucratic organizations and must be remedied by changing the structure of the organization and the mindset of everyone in it.

At least one hotel chain has done just that, as the following case illustrates.

Pull up to the Marriott Hotel in Schaumburg, Illinois, and you'll be met by a multi-talented GSA (guest service associate) who will greet you, sign you into the hotel, get your key, take your bags to the room, and take care of any special needs you might have. The GSA can even arrange tickets to a play or make reservations at a favorite restaurant. Says one GSA, "I'm a bellman, a doorman, a front-desk clerk, and a concierge all rolled into one. I have more responsibilities. I feel better about my job, and the guests get better service." At this hotel, guests now make it from curb to room in as *little as three minutes, down from ten to fifteen under the old system.*[6]

In addition to re-orchestrating the way jobs are divided up, this hotel makes a great effort to change the mindset of its employees. New hires at the hotel participate in an extensive training period. Each is assigned a mentor, or "buddy," responsible for fixing in their minds the goals of first-class service. Then, they take refresher courses over a three-month period. In addition, everyone works hard as a team to promote a culture of excellence in service to the guests. The same principle has been applied in early child care programs. One team, for example, organized its members around a holistic approach, working together to meet all the needs of each child.

> We worked hard to become a team. That meant we had to shift our thinking. We had to begin looking at our own little piece as part of a whole picture. That meant we had to follow the whole child. For example, our health person doesn't just look at health-she looks at education and enrollment and tries to integrate them. When following the child through our system, we can see how everybody's part fits into the agency's whole. It is hard, and there is still some residue of the old way of thinking. It takes time for some people to embrace change.

Two Basic Changes Needed to Bring about Team Management

These examples show the two key elements of team management. First, the structure of the organization is designed to disseminate power, making each person responsible for a larger portion of the work. Everyone is empowered to find solutions to problems in many areas. Second, much of the team's effort is dedicated to creating a culture, or mindset, of excellence and service. Individuals become responsible to the team, rather than to a boss, for carrying into action this collective way of thinking.

In the chapters that follow, we will use actual case histories to show how child care organizations can promote both the culture and the structure of team management. The process of change will not be easy, but we promise that it will be rewarding. Child care organizations are ideally suited to this new form of management.

Chapter Application Exercises
A. Personal Inventory: Leadership Self Evaluation

1. Are the people who work under your direction mainly: a) someone to help you get your work done? b) someone that you hope to mentor and assist in developing his or her full potential? c) someone who should make you look good to your own boss?

2. When people seem to be reluctant to do what you believe needs to be done, do you: a) get them to follow your directions by making the consequences painful? b) get them to follow your will by finding ways to make it worth their while? c) look for ways to help them decide from within that it is a worthwhile thing to do? d) work together to determine what needs to be done, and then work with them to find the best way to do it?

3. When you give someone an assignment, do you: a) check fre-

quently on them to make sure they are doing it correctly? b) leave it up to them as to how and when to do it? c) give them the freedom to find the best way, but expect them to return within a specified time to report their accomplishments?

4. In which of the following do you spend the most time: a) teaching people how to do their jobs; b) making sure they do what they have been assigned; c) solving problems for them; d) helping people see the larger picture of how their action will help or hurt children and families.

B. Group Exercise: Identifying Different Types of Organizations and Organizational Leaders

Instructions: Work in groups, or with at least one other individual, to discuss the following items. (Be ready to discuss or turn in your best examples):

1. Briefly describe an organization you have worked with (or had at least some contact with) that could best be described as one characterized by cronyism.

2. Describe the most bureaucratized organization you have ever worked or dealt with.

3. What organization are you familiar with that best fits the model of team leadership? What was it like and how motivated are staff there?

4. Describe a boss or leader you have known that best fits the transactional type.

5. Briefly describe a boss or leader that best fits the transformational type.

Chapter Notes

1. Accounts like this one were obtained from confidential interviews with program directors, teachers, and other early childhood leaders during 2002. Names will not me used to protect their anonymity.

2. Based on Alvin Gouldner, *Patterns of Industrial Bureaucracy* (New York: Free Press of Clencoe, 1954.

3. Based on interview reported on page 24 in Ralph P. Hummel. *The Bureaucratic Experience* (Neew York: St. Martin's Press, 1977.

4. Hummel, *The Bureaucratic Experience*, pages 26 and 27.

5. For a good discussion of this distinction, see Roger Dean Duncan and Ed J. Pinegar, *Leadership for Saints* (American Fork, Utah: Covenant Communications, 2002)

6. From Ronald Henkoff, "Finding, Training, and Keeping the Best Service workers," Fortune (October 31, 1994.

Chapter 2.
"Pushing the Right Buttons."
Motivation at the Individual Level

Chapter Summary

In this chapter, several forms of *intrinsic* motivation (e.g., feeling part of an important cause, belonging to a team, feeling a sense of ownership, and the importance of high expectations) are compared to *extrinsic* forms of motivation (rewards and/or punishment). The advantages and pitfalls of each are illustrated.

Introduction

One boss, after hearing a lot about team leadership, decided to make the change.

> I thought I could just "turn on" the new behavior like you turn on a light bulb. If only it were that simple. So, I hired a consultant to help me. His conclusion was devastating. "You are the problem," the consultant told me. "You prevent people from really doing their jobs. You dominate meetings. You give your own solutions—sometimes even before the problem is raised. You finish other people's sentences. You state your opinions first. Who's going to argue with you? You cut people off. You change agendas during the meeting, raising issues no one else is prepared to discuss. People leave meetings feeling discouraged rather than energized. You insist on making every decision. No wonder people don't take responsibility. You won't let them".[1]

For many administrators, becoming a team leader isn't easy. The idea of being a boss is deeply ingrained. In our schools, it is how our teachers got us to work when we were children. Most organizations rely on it to get employees to do their jobs. So, it's difficult for many bosses to become team leaders. But, change they must.

Types of Personal Motivation in School Programs

In schools and work organizations, the old boss-style management creates enormous motivation problems. In the last chapter, we saw that bureaucracies rely on external control (the old "carrot and stick" approach) to get things done. In bureaucratized schools, students have to be pushed and threatened. The most motivated ones frequently start working for grades, rather than for true understanding. Schools where students love learning dramatically outperform schools that rely on the carrots and sticks of grades and punishments. In bureaucratized businesses, employees often do their jobs only if some threat or reward is forthcoming. That's just not good enough in today's competitive world. Companies with employees who really care about customers are taking over entire markets.

Most early childhood programs can't pay their child care professionals enough to compete with better-paying jobs. They need child care professionals who are motivated from within (often called intrinsic motivation). These child care professionals care about helping children and are concerned about low-income families. Money is not their primary motivation. They work because they know they really can make a difference.

The box $(2.1)^2$ tells the story of a man motivated by his desire to save starfish. He did not make this effort because of pay or fear of personal consequences. He was motivated by love and concern for life. Most teachers in school programs similarly get great satisfaction from making a difference "for that one." That type of motivation cannot be purchased.

But intrinsic motivation can be stifled by either autocratic or bureaucratic bosses. Many teachers who are deeply motivated by their desire to help children become frustrated when

---

Box 2.1

One At A Time

An American walking on a deserted Mexican beach spotted a man in the distance. As he got closer, he saw a Mexican man picking up starfish that had washed up on the beach and throwing them back into the ocean. When he asked for an explanation, he was told that the starfish would die on the beach for lack of oxygen. "I understand," said the American, "but there are thousands of starfish on the beach, and there are thousands of other beaches with their thousands. Can't you see that you can't possibly make a difference? The native smiled, threw another starfish into the ocean, and said, "Made a difference for that one".

The same sentiment was expressed by a former Secretary-General of the United Nations, Dag Hammarskjold, who said, "It is more noble to give yourself completely to one individual than to labor diligently for the salvation of the masses."

someone else tries to control their work and make decisions without any consultation. This is a key element in the "burnout" experienced by some individuals who work in social welfare agencies (including Head Start).

Our discussion so far has identified two major types of personal motivation—intrinsic, or internalization, and external, or extrinsic. There is an in-between form, called identification. These three types are illustrated in the accompanying figure.

As the 2.1 figure illustrates, external, or extrinsic, motivation is the classic "carrot and stick" approach and the one most common in boss-style bureaucracies. Identification, the second type, occurs when individuals feel strong attachment to a group. They accept the group standards, not because they have a strong commitment to the standards, but because they believe in the group. Children often are motivated by identification, accepting things their parents believe in because of their identification with them. With time, they frequently internalize these beliefs and accept them as their own. For this reason, identification is usually a significant step in bringing about the third type, intrinsic motivation, which results from the process of internalization. Intrinsic motivation, as the name suggests, comes from within. It includes all forms of motivation that individuals have taken in, or internalized, from their families, social groups, or society.

Figure 2.1

Three Forms of Personal Motivation
1. External (extrinsic) – Use of positive incentives or negative sanctions
2. Identification – Use of identification with a group to get individual to accept their standards
3. Internalization (intrinsic) – Individuals internalize (accept as their own) group standards and regulate their own behavior

Internalization is a very powerful form of motivation. The following two descriptions illustrate this.

Case 1—A Prison Convict. I'd only been in prison ten days when I saw my first stabbing. A guy just dropped at my feet in San Quentin's main yard with a knife sticking out of his back. Everybody else was "con wise," smart enough to know what was going on. I didn't. All 6,000 guys were looking someplace else. Nobody saw anything, except me, and I'm right in the middle of the circle looking at the guy who was stabbed.

And so the "bulls" grabbed me (a guard is called a "hack," or a "bull," or a "screw.") They took me to an isolated treatment cell. The guard said, "You saw this knife used in the stabbing, didn't you. Who did it?" For nineteen days, they tried to make me talk. Then, they threw me back out. Convicts picked me up. Convicts helped in the jute mill. And every time a convict helped me, he risked the same punishment I had just undergone.

I'm still a convict, though I'm out of prison. I'm no more a stool pigeon now than I was then, and I don't like stool pigeons. In a girls' boarding school, they're called tattletales. In the Army, they're called traitors, and they shoot them.[3]

Case 2.—A Nineteenth-Century University President. Place me behind prison walls—walls of stone ever so high, ever so thick, reaching ever so far into the ground--there is a possibility that in some way or another I may be able to escape; but stand me on the floor and draw a chalk line around me and have me give my word of honor never to cross it. Can I get out of that circle? No, never! I'd die first.

The first of these examples is interesting because it shows that even people we often consider "unmotivated" will endure extreme punishment to uphold an ideal. In this case, the internalized belief indicates that it is wrong to "squeal" on fellow convicts. The man speaking endured brutal punishment rather than violate his internalized standards.

The second case may seem out of date in today's "Me First" world, because the individual speaking would deprive himself of liberty rather than violate his word of honor. Still, we can find many examples of such intense internalization today, including mothers who would not only die for their children but who would sacrifice a great deal of personal freedom to rear them. Internalization is still a very powerful form of motivation. It not only creates powerful motivation, but individuals regulate their own behavior without being prodded, rewarded, or externally motivated.

If internalization is such a powerful and effective form of individual motivation, why is it not used in organizations? Actually, it is, though not very often. Several companies in Japan, for example, have no cashiers in their cafeterias. Individuals leave what they owe in a box, and take out their own change (with little money ever lost through theft). In some parts of the United States, copy centers exist where people make their own copies and pay what they owe in much the same fashion. Some organizations have succeeded in making internalization their primary form of motivating folks. Staff in these organizations voluntarily put in a great deal of overtime, even though they are not paid for it, and no one requires or even notices it. They, like the individuals mentioned above, have internalized values and standards by which they govern their own behavior.

Often, however, bureaucracy gets in the way and even stifles internal motivation, as the following case illustrates.

Leader of Sign Crew: When I first joined the traffic department, I felt I knew my job. My job was taking out my crew—I had two helpers—go out with the truck, and we'd see a street sign down, and we'd put it back up. We had all kinds of signs in the truck. We'd do maybe 40 signs a day. Then, they said: "Put it on paper." So, we did maybe 35 signs or so, and the rest was paperwork. I guess if

it wasn't on paper, they didn't feel it was done. Then, they brought
in an efficiency expert. The section boss one morning hands me
a piece of paper: "You will put up this and this many signs a day,
or we'll know the reason why." I looked at the piece of paper and
took it out in the street to my crew. We rolled in the street for 20
minutes, laughing our heads off. Their quota was 20 signs a day.
We'd been doing 30, 40 before they started screwing around. . . .
Paperwork, reports, efficiency experts! Now, we do 20 signs and
knock off.[4]

Bureaucracy, or boss-style management, is the major form of motivation used in most organizations for a variety of reasons. One reason, as mentioned earlier, is that many managers or administrators don't
know any other way. Another major factor, however, is the enticement
that bureaucratic control offers, with its many external controls (rules,
top-down authority, and specialization of tasks). If administrators and
managers believe that staff members are basically unmotivated, they
will use bureaucratic (boss style) management to get them to work. This
seems to be the situation in the case just mentioned about the sign repair
crew.

Unfortunately, this mistrust becomes a self-fulfilling prophecy—we
act on the belief that workers are unmotivated. As a result, they become
unmotivated. People tend to live up to the expectations we have of them.
If a manager does not trust her staff, they may become undependable and
will then need constant monitoring. We see this in schools where too
many external controls produce students who will do little work unless
rewarded or threatened with punishment. Many bureaucratic organizations are likewise filled with staff who do only what they have to, complain if asked to do more, and turn aside from fixing urgent problems
because "it's not required by my job." This is illustrated by the following account given to us by a home visitor.

Because of my training as a social worker, I am used to working
with people in crisis. When a parent called me just before closing
time on a Friday afternoon and told me that she was going to kill
herself, I took her seriously. I called my supervisor to notify her.
I was stunned when she told me not to worry about it. "There is
no way she's going to commit suicide on a Friday afternoon," she
told me. When I got off the phone with her, I called her supervisor, knowing that I could get into a lot of trouble. But, I was really
worried about this family. Fortunately, I got the support I needed
for the family, and it was worth the risk.

This tendency to disassociate oneself from anything outside one's
job description (or, in the preceding case, outside working hours) is fairly
common in many bureaucratized organizations. It reveals another reason
why this self-fulfilling prophecy of "unmotivated worker" is common in
such organizations. You will recall that bureaucracies tend to break work
down into many parts, with each individual only responsible for a small

part of the overall work of the organization. Consequently, remedying problems becomes someone else's job. Individual workers lose their sense of what the organization is all about. James A. Belasco and Ralph C. Stayer, the authors of a marvelous book, Flight of the Buffalo, describe a visit by a consultant to the president of a $6 billion company.

As they were walking around the corporate headquarters, they passed a groundskeeper who was raking leaves with a broken rake. It had only five of its original thirty-one teeth. As a result, it was picking up hardly any leaves. So they stopped and asked her why she was using a broken rake that was not picking up any leaves. She responded that she was using it because it was what she had been given. When they asked her why she didn't get a better rake, she replied, "That's not my job."

The corporate executive was angry and told the consultant that this example showed the lack of a sense of urgency he had just mentioned. He said. "How are we ever going to make it if we can't even give someone a decent rake? I've got to find that supervisor and be certain she gets a better rake."

The consultant asked him if he was sure that her supervisor was the person responsible. The executive was emphatic in blaming the supervisor, stating that it was every supervisor's job to make sure his people had the right equipment. So the consultant asked what he could do to solve the problem of supervisors not giving proper equipment. The leader thought about it for a minute and then decided that he would set a good example by going himself to get the gardener a new rake. When the consultant asked if that would really fix the problem, the president thought for a moment before saying, "If every person in this company doesn't get a sense of urgency about meeting their commitments, we aren't going to make it."

Next, the consultant asked, "If everyone must be committed to doing their jobs no matter what it takes, then who must take responsibility in the case of the gardener and the rake?" Finally, the president saw the point—the gardener had to be responsible. She was the only one who could be certain that she had the right rake. In fact, each person had to be responsible for their own performance. Still, the president was puzzled. Somehow he still felt that the supervisor needed to be more responsible. The consultant explained that the supervisor was responsible for getting the groundskeeper committed to doing a good job, but not for getting her the right rake.

Finally the consultant asked the president to consider who else needed to be committed to getting the right rake. After thinking about it for a minute, he realized that many people had probably seen the gardener using the wrong rake. If they were concerned about results, they should have spoken up. Every person needed to feel responsible for making sure that the gardener got the right rake.

(Based on Bellasco and Stayer, 1993:43-4)

As this account illustrates, bureaucratic organizations tend to produce staff who dutifully go through the motions of their work without thinking about the overall effect of their performance. When the products they provide seldom change (i.e., a factory), such specialization might work well. A factory that produces the same product over and over doesn't need each worker always trying to innovate. People just have to do their part over and over. But, when an organization deals with new situations all the time, everyone needs to be a problem solver, and everyone needs to promote the overall success of the organization. Rules developed for one purpose, if rigidly applied, may defeat the overall mission of the organization, as the following case illustrates.

> Our center has to operate under the Federal Guidelines of the Head Start Performance Standards. One of these standards reads that children must be held while being bottle-fed. Because we have a rule against holding children older than nine months during feeding, our Director told us to start weaning babies from the bottle by the time they were nine months old. That certainly didn't help the babies, and I'm sure it wasn't what the standards were trying to accomplish.

Team leadership is a new approach to motivation. People work more in teams and "cross train" so that each individual knows how to do the work of other positions. This tends to break down the isolationist attitude that "it's not my job." It also works to reduce goal displacement, or becoming so enmeshed in one's own duties that the overall purposes of the organization are forgotten. And finally, team leadership allows people to experience esprit de corps as they work together to accomplish something really important. These elements are evident in the following description of Southwest Airlines, a company whose practice of team leadership set new standards for the airline industry.

> Southwest Airlines began as a small airline in 1971 with only 198 employees. Since then, its team approach has resulted in the number-one ranking for on-time flights, with fares among the lowest in the industry. Employees are trained for specific jobs, but each is expected to help other employees when the need arises, and they are able to do so. Pilots, for example, are frequently seen helping with luggage, or even with cleaning, so that flights will leave on time. Pilots are team leaders, but the entire team is responsible for getting flights out on time, with excellent service and low cost.
>
> Each team member is responsible for spotting problems before they occur and finding solutions. Through regular cross-training, each teammate knows the duties of other team members. Great emphasis is placed on open communications, rather than waiting for the "person in charge" to say what needs to be done. Even top executives expect to receive occasional experience in lowly tasks. Indeed, the evaluation of pilots includes not only their skills at piloting an aircraft, but also how well they can involve team members in good decisions that improve efficiency, safety, and customer satisfaction. Many observers thought this family-like culture could not last as the

airline expanded. But the airline has grown well beyond 11,000 employees and still maintains its close-knit culture and its innovative team structure.[5]

Four Sources of Intrinsic Motivation

While it may be easy to see that intrinsic motivation is superior to the excessive use of external motivation so common in boss-style organizations, it is much more difficult to put into practice. Child care professionals and managers are accustomed to doing things the old way. Some resist change because it is uncomfortable, and they don't want to be responsible for more than their own little niche. But most people become supportive when they experience the exhilaration of working together in teams, when they don't have to check their minds at the door, and when they find great satisfaction in being part of an outstanding effort to advance a noble cause.

The example of Southwest Airlines helps us illustrate several fundamental forms of intrinsic motivation. Specifically, these are: commitment to an important cause, feeling part of a valued group, gaining a sense of ownership for something really worthwhile, and experiencing high expectations from someone we really respect. Let's analyze each and examine how they can dramatically improve the motivation of child care professionals and parents in early childhood programs.

A. Commitment to an Important Cause

The story is told of a man traveling in a distant country. He came upon a very large and impressive construction project. Naturally, he was curious and wanted to know what was being built. He found a man at work on the project and asked, "What is this project you're doing?" The laborer looked at him like he was dense and replied, "Can't you see? I'm laying bricks." Naturally, this didn't satisfy the traveler's curiosity, so he stopped another laborer, with much the same result. "Can't you see, I'm building a wall." Unwilling to let it go, he stopped a third laborer with the same question. This time, he got what he was looking for. Said the laborer with pride, "I'm building a mighty temple to my God."

Each of the laborers in this parable was doing the same work, laying bricks for the wall of a temple. But, each had a very different sense of the cause in which he was engaged. Child care professionals in school programs are much the same. Some are only "laying bricks," just putting in time and going through the motions. Others envision a bit more long range and consider themselves as part of an important program. Still others have a deeper sense of what they are about.

Like the Mexican saving starfish on the beach, they see a much greater cause. They are helping highly vulnerable children overcome great obstacles to really become something. Their cause is to develop the minds of children to help them rise above the difficult circumstances of poverty.

As you can imagine, these child care professionals are the ones who aren't in it for the money. They find great satisfaction in a job that offers few external rewards.

Why don't all child care professionals equally appreciate this great cause? In fact, most probably do, at least some of the time. Here again, bureaucracy is part of the problem. If they are told what to do, monitored much of the time, treated as a cog in a larger wheel, and allowed little voice in making their program operate better, most will inevitably lose sight of the cause. Increasingly, they will view themselves as bricklayers, rather than as temple builders.

It doesn't have to be like that. If Southwest Airline employees can work together to be enthusiastic about the cause of customer satisfaction, how much more potential do early childhood programs have to build a powerful sense of purpose? This is one of the real advantages of this line of work. We need to help each other see that what we are doing matters far more, in the long term, than producing a new brand of toothpaste or making flights arrive on time.

We need each other to keep this perspective. It is difficult not to get bogged down in detail. Every team meeting should bring us back to the cause. We all need to lift the vision of each other and share successes in making a difference for the children under our care. We may not be able to save all the children, but we should help each other see, on a daily basis, that our collective effort "made a difference for that one."

B. Feeling Part of a Valued Group

During WWII, the American military often attempted to get German soldiers to surrender by distributing leaflets that revealed many of the horrible things Hitler was doing. They believed that German soldiers would surely give up if they knew how wrong their cause was. Nevertheless, no German soldiers surrendered as a result of this information. In fact, captured German POWs told the Americans of severely injured comrades who would sneak out of hospitals in order to rejoin their units. Moreover, the Americans found that many of the German soldiers already hated Hitler and the Nazi movement.

Why then didn't they surrender? Further investigation revealed that the German Army kept units together throughout the entire war. As a result, soldiers became intensely loyal to their buddies in these small, tightly-knit units. Thus, men would risk death to return to battle even when they didn't have to and in spite of the knowledge that the cause was unjust. They did so solely because they could not let their buddies down.

Group loyalty can be a powerful motivator. Often, however, bureaucratic management emphasizes formality in relationships. Managers are encouraged to keep their distance from staff in the belief that formality will keep decisions objective. While few among us want to go back to the pre-bureaucratic days of autocratic leadership, when hiring relatives and doing things on the basis of playing favorites was common, we lose an important element of motivation if relationships become too formal. Herb Kelleher, chairman of Southwest Airlines, for example, spent much of his time socializing with his employees and learning about their ideas. He held weekly cookouts where employees join with him to celebrate the company's success. He even had a well-known sense of humor that includes playing pranks on customers and employees (he has been known, for example, to dress up as Elvis Presley or the Easter Bunny). He encourages employees to display a sense of humor with passengers to enliven their flights. His employees felt a strong personal commitment to each other and willingly go the extra mile to support the goals of the airline.

It is important to point out, however, that happy employees are not necessarily more productive. Remember the gypsum plant mentioned in the first chapter? Workers were happy because they could take advantage of the company, and no one cared much about productivity. It's also a mistake to assume that employees who feel strong loyalty towards each other will be highly productive. Some organizations have problems with tight-knit staff who develop a culture that opposes productivity. Some work groups, for example, set a slow pace and punish any deviation from that pace with ostracism and label as "rate busters" those who want to work at a faster pace

The key to making group loyalty a major form of positive motivation is to make sure that tight-knit groups, as they form, support organizational goals. The best way to do this is to give staff the opportunity to help define these goals. When Herb Kelleher seeks out the opinions of Southwest employees, he not only benefits from their ideas—he also develops a sense of loyalty among those who sense that their input is valued. They feel part of the team. These teams can be a powerful force in tying group loyalty to the mission of the larger organization.

C. Developing Ownership in Something Really Worthwhile

A newly-hired high school teacher in a rural community was shocked to discover the deplorable condition of the building assigned for his classes. The problem was due to more than just a lack of funds, however. His school was often damaged by vandalism, much of which was done by the students.

One day the teacher told his students how people elsewhere in the state regarded their town as a joke. When the kids got angry, he said, "What do you expect? Anyone driving by this school would think people here prefer run-down, ugly buildings."

After some discussion, one of the students suggested they could fix up the small building used for his classes and asked for his help. "It's not my building," he said. "But if I can spare some time, I might help out occasionally." Students got someone to donate paint and even planted a lawn.

The teacher knew he had succeeded in building a sense of ownership when, one morning, he saw some other students walking on the newly-planted lawn. His own students chased them down! He had to restrain them from doing serious harm to the trespassers.

What a difference a feeling of ownership can make. Students who once vandalized the school now became its protectors. It had become their building.

How do organizations like schools and early childhood centers get employees to feel personally responsible for getting great results? If top management alone is interested in having the best on-time record in the industry, staff will do little to make it happen. Everyone needs to be committed to attaining this goal. People who feel ownership for a problem will go to great lengths to find a good solution.

Still, ownership can be de-motivating if our problems seem to have no solutions. Who wants to own the problem of child care professionals who cannot get along, or of people who badmouth co-workers behind their backs? Even so, ownership is generally a positive motivator. People derive satisfaction from creating something valuable. We are pleased when we solve difficult problems. As we share that journey with people we care about, it is doubly motivating, as the following case from one center illustrates.

> We recently moved into a new building. Our executive director asked one staff member to set up the communication system for the whole building. This included telephones, internet, networking throughout our entire three-county agency. The WHOLE thing! Though he was a bit intimidated, he accepted. He got really excited and wanted to do a good job for everyone. He was given a lot of latitude to do it. Often, problems came up, and we frequently had to all get together and rethink things. At first, he felt like he was letting us down. Someone said, "Let's just pull up our socks and try again." We kept meeting with him as a team and if something didn't work, we'd get back together, find out what went wrong, and suggest ways to fix it. Once he realized we were all fine with how he was doing and not mad or feeling like he'd let us down, he worked very hard. He didn't quit until we got a really great system.

As this account illustrates, individuals are much more likely to take ownership when they feel supported by a team. This includes letting people take calculated risks without feeling like they will be punished if there are occasional failures.

In many agencies, managers and administrators often feel they are the only ones feeling this sense of ownership. Front-line staff commonly are the first to see a problem, yet believe it is the administrator's job to find a solution. If the administrator is a good problem solver, he or she will own all the problems. No one else will feel responsible. The gardener with the broken rake, for example, felt no sense of ownership for the problem of a broken rake.

In such cases, boss-style management is the problem. According to this arrangement, bosses should solve problems. Workers are supposed to do as they are told. However, this scheme robs employees of a sense of ownership. As a result, the organization suffers because people who see the problems first feel no obligation to find solutions.

Team management can change this. The team works together to define its mission and objectives. Team meetings are oriented toward finding better ways to do things and solving the problems they identify. This is what the team did for the individual asked to set up their communications system.

Empowerment is the key to ownership. Team members need to know that they are empowered to find better ways to do things. Bosses who want to hold on to power and who have to maintain control will have child care professionals with minimal commitment to the goals of the organization. Bosses need to become team leaders and give up being in control over everything. The best leaders are those who empower others to do great things and spend most of their time clearing the way for them to be successful. An end-of-chapter exercise will help you further examine how to go about doing so.

D. The Importance of Great Expectations

Perhaps the biggest difference in programs that successfully involve parents and those that do not is in their ability to expect great accomplishments. Comedian Flip Wilson used to say, "What you see is what you get." Program personnel who see low-income parents as uncooperative and uncaring will experience little cooperation and a great deal of apathy from parents. Those committed to finding the good in people will find it. They will also find it easier to have high expectations. What they see is, in fact, what they will get.

We are not talking about building self-esteem. That movement is often more of a manipulation than a genuine effort to raise our own expectations. Many of these parents have become very good at spotting fakery. Telling them we think they are great when they know we feel otherwise will only produce alienation. We have to truly believe in them because we have seen beyond the problems, the disappointments, and the frustrations to what they can still do well. If we don't see it, we won't get it.

This all requires a different form of relating to staff members and parents. We have to spend time with them, even when there are other pressing concerns. We must visit parents and community leaders in their homes. We should ask other child care professionals or parents to tell us about their strengths. We have to connect, and we have to see victories where we might otherwise see failures. The following case illustrates this point.

> I had this one staff member who was used to only doing one particular project. Our whole program is set up to be more multi-task oriented, however. I knew this man could do it, but he wasn't so sure. He needed a lot of guidance at first, and I made sure to spend time with him along the way. And with small steps and goals, I was gradually able

to let him go. You should see him now! His team is wonderful, and he has cultivated several very good child care professional members. He has presented our program regionally and even nationally. He use to speak real quiet and not often; now, he speaks with confidence.

Seeing the good in others in order to maintain high expectations is a key component of team leadership. If we don't trust parents or fellow child care professionals, we will never really empower them. We will not want them to be part of our team. Then, if we do not truly value the people we work with, our sense of feeling part of an important cause will suffer.

One category of parents for whom expectations are often minimal is low-income fathers. The image of "deadbeat dads" has become so entrenched in our society that it is difficult to avoid lowered expectations. Additionally, our culture subscribes to the idea that fathers do not want to be nurturers. Instead, such work is relegated to mothers. Two cases from the book, New Expectations: Community Strategies for Responsible Fatherhood,[6] will demonstrate just how low our expectations are for meaningful participation from fathers, and the negative consequences that follow.

Head Start Study. In 1990, the Department of Health and Human Services funded the most extensive and expensive study to date of "The Effects of Parent Participation on Head Start Parents and Children." The interview sample for this groundbreaking study, designed to help shape the future of Head Start, included over 1,000 parents, or more accurately, over 1,000 mothers. Not one father was interviewed. The operating assumption was that fathers were unavailable or uninterested or unimportant, or perhaps all three—that they had little to contribute to either their families or our understanding of how to make Head Start work better for children.

A Non-Sexist Center. In Great Britain, one school that prided itself on its non-sexist approach decided to demonstrate just how equally it treated all parents. Using videotapes, the director of the Pen Green Centre of Corby recorded the comings and goings of mothers and fathers on the playground, dropping off and picking up their children, and talking with child care professional. Before the experiment, the all-female child care professional claimed that it was gender-neutral in its approach. But, the tape revealed two totally different types of interaction. Child care professionals greeted mothers more frequently, both verbally and with waving or handshaking. Child care professionals initiated conversations more frequently with mothers and held longer conversations with mothers than with fathers. Before examining the videos, the child care professionals would have sworn they were equally respectful of both mothers' and fathers' connections to their children. Afterwards, they realized they had built very sturdy "on-ramps" for mothers and very rickety ones, at best, for fathers.

Levine and Pitt find that the participation of men in early childhood programs increases substantially when expectations are raised. "This," they say, "has proved to be true in prenatal outreach to low-income non-custodial fathers, in working with teenage fathers in school settings, and in working with fathers of all backgrounds." Raising expectations really can raise involvement and meaningful participation.

Motivating Parents and Our Target Community

To this point, our discussion of motivation has revolved around the issue of how we motivate child care professionals. For many school programs, dealing with low-income families is a bigger problem than motivating child care professionals. We need parents as volunteers. We need them to be motivated to do more for their children. Some seem to have given up hope and use our programs as an escape from being a parent for a few hours each day.

The principles of motivation outlined above work equally well for low-income parents. They also can be motivated by feeling part of an important cause, by being part of a valued group, and in feeling a sense of ownership. Programs that systematically employ these forms of motivation are highly successful in gaining the cooperation of parents. Those that do not often resort to paternalistic, boss-management style, then complain bitterly about selfish and unmotivated parents.

Let's briefly compare these two styles and their effects on low-income parents. Boss-style, or bureaucratic, programs keep some distance away from parents, interacting with them in a business-like relationship. Many parents will interpret this as aloofness on the part of the program and will certainly not see themselves as part of an important team, no matter how much we say they are needed. Since agency personnel are trained in childcare, they are seen as experts sent in to solve a problem. Many parents are more than happy to transfer ownership and wonder why the program keeps asking for their time.

On the other hand, team leadership programs regard parents as valuable resources, and treat them as such. They seek out ways to build relationships with parents. These programs create many opportunities to visit informally with parents and get to know them as more than someone dropping off a child. Over time, they are able to understand together the importance of the cause in which they are involved and rejoice together in each accomplishment they see in a child. One by one, they involve parents in councils and really empower these councils to make important decisions. Such programs transfer ownership of many problems to these councils and are willing to let them make some mistakes as they learn, without jerking back control at the first sign of failure.

Chapter Application Exercises
A. Personal Reflection Exercise: How much ownership?

As we begin to give greater ownership to those who work under our direction, we need to consider the readiness of each individual for additional responsibility. As you review the following levels[7], ask yourself which level best matches *your* current state of preparation. Then, mentally do the same for key individuals who work under your direction.

Level 1—Waits for instruction—Does only what he or she is told to do, and then only with considerable follow-up;

Level 2—Takes the initiative to ask what to do. Follows instructions and looks for ways to accomplish more (but only after given additional instructions);

Level 3—Suggests work or direction that might be needed—Is proactive in identifying things that need to be done, but still waits for authorization;

Level 4—Acts immediately, but reports action immediately to supervisor-No longer waits to be told what should be done, but wants immediate feedback;

Level 5—Acts immediately, but reports only during scheduled feedback opportunities-Now feels empowered to act, but still feels need for periodic feedback;

Level 6—Acts on whatever needs doing and moves on to other needed work-At this level the child care professional feels fully empowered and is not made to explain actions.

Further Thoughts: You might further consider that each person's level will vary by the type of responsibility being considered. Often, we are at one level for some responsibilities, but a higher or lower level for others. What responsibilities could be given at a higher level for some of the individuals you have just considered?

B. Group Exercise: Using the Three Forms of Motivation with Parents.
Instructions: Work in groups, or with at least one other individual, to answer the following questions. Be ready to discuss or turn in your results.

1. In thinking about the community you serve, what are the causes parents might consider important? How can these causes be tied to your program?

2. What steps could you take to make parents of children in your program have greater ownership for the success of your program?

3. What actions could you take to build a strong identification with a team among the parents of the children in your program?

Chapter Notes

-----

1. Adapted from James A. Belasco and Ralph C. Stayer, *Flight of the Buffalo: Soaring to Excellence, Learning to Let Employees Lead* (New York: Warner Books, 1993).

2. See Jack Canfield and Mark Victor Hansen, *Chicken Soup for the Soul* (Dearfield Beach, Florida: Health Communications, Incorporated, 1993). 22, 23.

3. Speech by Bill Sands, former convict of San Quentin Prison, to Lamar Community College, Lamar, Colorado. 1970.

4. Hummel, *The Bureaucratic Experience*, 93.

5. Summarized from Jennifer M. George and Gareth R. Jones, *Understanding and Managing Organizational Behavior* (Reading Mass.: Addison-Wesley Publishing Company, 1996). 2.

6. James A. Levine and Edward W. Pitt, *New Expectations: Community Strategies for Responsible Fatherhood* (New York: Families and Work Institute, 1995).

7. These levels are based, in part, on a similar set of labels suggested by Duncan and Pinegar. 210.

Chapter 3.
"The Power of the Situation:"
Motivation at the Organizational Level

Chapter Summary

In early childhood organizations, problems are caused more often by organizational structure than by personality clashes. Another organizational component, the collective "mindset" or organizational culture, can also create difficulties, especially problems of low motivation. The organizational structure and the organizational culture bring out the worst (or the best) in people. By changing key elements of each, you can improve commitment and efficiency. You can also create an environment in which everyone works to solve problems, thus making your agency much more effective.

Introduction

Behind the windows of a New York City housing project, hundreds of people were asleep or preparing for bed. Then, a piercing scream rent the night air. Curtains parted in nearby buildings as 38 residents of the project witnessed the brutal stabbing of a young woman.

As the assailant fled into the night, each witness felt grateful for the relative security of locked doors and the police they assumed would soon be on the scene. But no police arrived. No one rushed to the aid of the severely wounded woman. In fact, several minutes later the assailant returned to finish the job.[1]

As this story came to light, people were shocked—not only at the fact that a woman had been brutally murdered, but more so that no one had helped her. None of the witnesses even called the police. It was asked, "What is becoming of places like New York City? Doesn't anyone care any more?"

The Power of the Situation

Actually, many of those who witnessed the murder did care. The nature of the social situation in which it occurred seems to have affected their lack of action, possibly even more than the personalities of the people involved. Witnesses knew what was happening. Each could see, however, that many other people also knew. Each person apparently assumed that with so many other witnesses, someone would certainly offer aid or call the police. As a result, none of them did.

Following the public outcry over the apparently callous reaction seen in this case, two researchers decided to investigate whether something other than insensitivity was at work. They suspected that the nature of social situations, rather than some personality flaw, determines whether individuals render aid to others. They set up an experiment in a public place, making it appear that someone was having a seizure. Each time, varying numbers of other people were present. As it turned out, the number of bystanders was the most important factor related to whether anyone offered help. Essentially, the fewer the bystanders, the more likely it was that assistance would be given.[2]

Other experiments have demonstrated the same principle. The structure of social situations, and the collective mindset that is created in organizations, have powerful effects on human behavior. One more case will illustrate this.

Research psychologist, Stanley Milgram,[3] wanted to determine how much pain people would inflict upon someone else if a person in authority told them to do so. Obviously, experiments in which dangerous pain is actually administered would be considered morally wrong, so Milgram decided to make people **think** that they were inflicting pain. He designed an apparatus that looked very much like an electrical shock generator. He then told people he would pay them to participate as "teachers" in a scientific experiment designed to measure the effects of punishment on learning.

People were told that a "learner" in another room was connected to the electrical apparatus. If this person made an error in memory recall, the teacher was to give the learner a shock by flipping a switch on the control panel. Actually, the learner in the other room was an actor who never received any real shocks, but acted as if he had. As the actor kept on making errors, the teachers were told to increase shock up to a level marked "450 volts" on the fake control panel.

When the "shocks" reached a high level, the actor would pound on the wall as if in great pain. If the teachers protested, they were ordered to go on, having been told that the experimenter would take full responsibility. Many teachers protested, but fully 65 percent of them continued to administer what they thought was a shock strong enough to kill someone. Even the one-third who would not go all the way administered what they thought was a shock that would cause extreme pain and suffering.

This experiment teaches us a lot about how people are motivated. Our inner motivation is greatly influenced by forces in our external social environment. While most people recognize that particular social situations exert some influence on individual actions, they typically believe that differences in human behavior are due to personality, inner motivations, or some hierarchy of needs. Here we see that the way relationships are "structured" also significantly impacts the psychological motivation of individuals. Milgram obtained his dramatic results by the way he structured the relationship of his "teacher" to himself and to the "learner" in the other room. He also strongly influenced their behavior by the way he got them to define this situation, or the shared mindset he created.

These two powerful factors need to be understood if they are to be forces for good in early childhood organizations. Let's examine each factor briefly, then demonstrate how early childhood organizations can benefit from the impact of each of these factors on individual behavior.

The Structure of the Situation. One of the great discoveries of social psychology (a cross between sociology and psychology) is that human behavior and our feelings depend, to a great extent, on the structure of our social situations. Kitty Genovese, the young woman murdered in New York City, was a victim not only of her attacker but also of the structure of her situation. The number of onlookers worked against anyone feeling sufficiently responsible to report the situation or to attempt stopping her attacker. Likewise, Milgram structured the situation in his experiment in a way that exercised a powerful influence on choices made by the "teachers." He created a relationship in which a person in authority took responsibility for the actions of each "teacher." He also put them in an employer-employee relationship because they agreed to be paid. Milgram kept the "learner" in another room, reducing teachers' contact so they felt little personal attachment and did not have to see the learner suffering.

Finally, he gradually increased the "shocks" so that each decision was only a small amount above what had already been done. By giving relationships a particular structure, he was able to produce an outcome that surprised even the most cynical predictions.

More than fifty years ago, Kurt Lewin demonstrated the importance of the way we "structure" relationships when he performed experiments on groups of boys. He found that the way authority was arranged in these groups, more than the personality of their leaders, was responsible for the productivity and cohesiveness of the groups. A relaxed, lassaiz-faire leadership was the least productive. Next was the highly regimented, authoritarian structure. Lewin's most productive and cohesive groups were more democratic ones in which leaders promoted team management and got everyone working together to set and accomplish group goals.

Lewin and other social psychologists have shown that the structure of a situation not only affects behavior directly, but also has a powerful influence on the process of internalization (discussed in Chapter Two). In other words, the way our programs are structured can have a powerful direct effect on our staff. This structure can also indirectly affect behavior by the way it promotes or hinders internalization.

This insight is good news for managers and program directors because it gives them additional ways to motivate their child care professionals and parents. The structure of relationships they create will directly affect people. Additionally, structure can be used to get child care professionals and parents to internalize key attitudes, values, and beliefs. We will shortly point out some of the most important ways of doing this. Before doing so, however, let's look at the other way situations affect us-through our cultural definitions of the situation.

The Definition of the Situation. Early in the last century, W. I. Thomas proposed that people responded less to reality and more to how they perceive it. This idea was called "the definition of the situation," or, as some prefer, the Thomas Theorum. Let's illustrate with a quick personal example provided by Carol Tavris in her book, *Anger: The Misunderstood Emotion.*[4]

> One afternoon, as I was leaving the subway at rush hour, trudging tiredly up the stairs, I felt a hand brush my rear. It was an ambiguous gesture, considering the size of the crowd, so I did nothing: but my heart began to pound and my face flushed. I felt a mixture of excitement (my first New York pervert!) and fury (how dare this creep molest me). The hand struck again, this time unmistakably a pinch. I spun around, umbrella poised to strike a blow for womanhood and self respect. . . . and stared face-to-face at my husband. He took one look at my apoplectic expression and burst out laughing, which was a good thing, as I might have whomped him anyhow. This example shows the speed with which a single judgment—"This man is a friend with a rotten sense of humor, not a pervert"—transformed my apprehension and anger into delight.

This story demonstrates that an interpretation of a situation, more than the situation itself, determined the reaction. Thus, not so much the pinch as how she defined or interpreted it, determined Tavris' reaction. We see this also in the failure of banks during the Great Depression. Their failure was caused more by the collective definition that the banks were weak than by how strong or weak the banks actually were. When everyone defines banks as unstable institutions that are about to fail, they will rush down to withdraw their money. As a result, banks will be severely threatened. Understanding this principle at the depth of the Depression, Franklin D. Roosevelt remarked, in his 1933 Inaugural Address, ". . . .the only thing we have to fear is fear itself."

Similarly, in your organization, the way people collectively define situations will exert a powerful influence on their behavior. In some organizations, anyone who does more than the average is defined as a "rate buster," and the group finds ways to get them to do less. In other organizations, people who do more than the average are recognized and appreciated. They serve as a model others want to follow. The difference is in how people in these organizations collectively define such behavior. We call these collective definitions of situations the organizational mindset, or the organizational culture.

Organizational culture powerfully influences behavior. In the preceding chapter, for example, we looked at how the organizational culture collectively defines the role of fathers. Are fathers really expected to participate as nurturers or caregivers in your center? A man who gets down with the children and finds everyone staring at him will come to see his own behavior as strange and will not likely be back to help. On the other hand, when the organizational culture regards such behavior as normal and expected, it will become much more common. Expectations are a powerful form of the collective definition of various situations in your organization.

Situational Leadership

Team management is a wonderful tool to build a positive organizational culture. It also provides a coherent structure that harnesses the power of situation in early childhood programs. Its unique structure and organizational culture can have a powerful influence on individuals, especially in getting them to internalize commitment to an important cause, feel part of a valued group, and gain a sense of ownership for something really worthwhile (the forms of internal motivation discussed in Chapter Two).

As we indicated in that chapter, team leadership takes time to build. Much of your work will be spent in building the abilities of team members toward becoming productive members of the team. This will require a lot of one-on-one time with them. And because each individual will not be equally prepared, you will need to vary the type of leadership you provide to each team member. This focused one-on-one leadership has been called "situational leadership."[5]

The basic idea of **situational leadership** is to alter your leadership efforts to match each individual's commitment and competence. Though most people recognize that we all have different levels of **commitment** and **competence**, it's amazing how we sometimes try to direct everyone with the same approach. By **commitment** we mean the level of a person's intrinsic motivation and their dedication to accomplishing tasks. We use the term **competence** to refer to a person's level of knowledge, skills, and abilities that are needed to accomplish assigned tasks.

Since an individual can be high on one of these and low on the other, there are a number of possible combinations of competence and commitment. This might best be illustrated by creating a grid with a person's level of competence on the horizontal axis, and their level of commitment on the vertical axis. If we apply the basic idea of situational leadership to this grid, we can see that the leadership role we take should correspond to where people are on the grid. This is shown in the following illustration: (3.1)

Figure 3.1

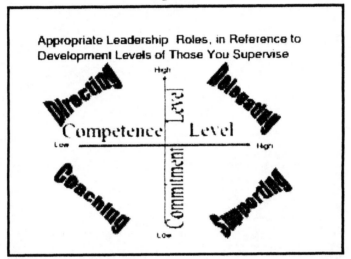

Individuals who are new to an organization often lack competence. They may also be low in commitment. Regardless of *why* someone may be low in competence and commitment, this type of person will require a lot of coaching, either by you or by team members. **Coaching** is working with an individual to build competence and motivation. It may require considerable skill training. It will also involve support from the team to instill the forms of intrinsic motivation described in Chapter Two.

When someone has a higher level of competence but is still low in motivation, situational leadership calls for a **supporting** leadership role. Supporting requires little skill building, but should help build a stronger level of commitment by again applying the major forms of intrinsic motivation.

When someone has a high level of motivation but is low in competence, your role will require a lot of **directing**. This may necessitate a more structured learning situation, with closer supervision as this individual learns necessary skills. Because of the high level of motivation, however, you will need to be available for answering a lot of questions, but will not need to supervise in a way that might convey a lack of trust. People in this situation need direction-but they do not need someone pushing them to work harder.

When individuals are high in both competence and motivation, your relationship with them should be very different from the other forms of situational leadership. Such persons will best be served by **delegating** many responsibilities to them that afford considerable authority to do things without first asking you for permission. You can turn many tasks over to them and require very little "reporting back." This can be a pleasant experience for you and for the person to whom you delegate responsibility. The most difficult aspect of that kind of arrangement will probably be to relinquish delegated assignments so that you empower such individuals to take full ownership for the responsibilities you have delegated to them.

Much of the supporting, coaching, directing, and delegating you enact personally will be tied in many ways to the organizational culture and structure you are trying to create. This is because, the way you structure your organization, and the shared culture you develop, will be two of your most powerful tools, to develop competence and build commitment. Let's look briefly at each of these, structure and culture, to see how they can be used to allow you to strengthen individuals in your organization.

The Organizational Structure Needed for Team Management

Every organization has a unique structure—the way the "parts" that people play fit together. An organization's structure describes how the different positions in the organization are set up in relation to each other. They can be related in terms of ranking (which positions have the most power), division of labor (which positions are responsible for what duties), and such things as the size of each part of the organization, the lines of communication, and how interconnected these divisions are. Understanding structure is more than an academic exercise. The particular way you structure your organization will have a powerful effect on the behavior of everyone in it. Let's examine the structure of organizations that use team management to illustrate.

Several structural conditions are needed for team management to really work. **First, organizations using this management style are not as hierarchical in their power structure as are bureaucracies.** Bosses become team leaders. Group decisions begin to replace autocratic top-down decisions. A team approach is more about working together in a spirit of camaraderie than is customary in the old boss-style management scheme, where one person makes decisions for others to execute. Extensive research has shown that people are much more likely to carry out decisions that they have had a part in making.

This was shown in a classic experiment conducted in 1947. Alfred Marrow and John French, students of Kurt Lewin, carried out an investigation in a single factory in which the staff members were divided into three groups. During the experiment, two men tried three different ways of making and implementing a decision.

With the initial group of staff members, a decision was first made by top leaders, then was announced to the other staff members in a meeting. The result followed the normal pattern. There was a lot of grumbling, production rates fell 20 percent, and the union began to oppose the change.

Among the second group of staff members were asked to select representatives to work with managers to decide the best way to make the changes. Though their decision was the same as the first group, there was much less opposition. Production soon returned to the previous level.

In the third group, however, all employees were asked to participate in the decision about the change and how to implement it. This group made the change and returned to their previous level of productivity in only two days. Furthermore, within two weeks their level of production increased 14 percent beyond its previous level and stayed there.

Under team management, leaders give up a considerable degree of power, turning many decisions over to the team. This is the point of the title of Belasco and Stayer's book, *Flight of the Buffalo*. A herd of buffalo has a leader and all will follow, even if it means running over a cliff. A flock of geese, on the other hand flies in a "V" formation, with the leader frequently falling back and another goose taking the lead. Thus, the emphasis of this work indicates that, when working with people who are accustomed to behaving like buffalo, we should help them learn to act as geese, or achieve team management—hence, the "flight of the buffalo."

One program, for example, had a Health Coordinator who was used to being involved only in decisions about health concerns. Her lack of ownership for all aspects of the program was obvious by the way she talked. In speaking to the Director, for example, she would always say "your program," or "your kids." As she became more involved in helping solve problems in other areas of the program, however, she began talking about "our program" and "our kids."

A second structural feature of team management is that its division of responsibilities becomes much more *cooperative* in nature. Rather than the highly specialized assembly-line type division of labor, people have broader work responsibilities and frequently help each other to get the job done. Cooperation, rather than isolation in one's own little sphere, becomes the way to get things done.

A closely related result is that work becomes organized around processes more than functions. For example, the Marriott hotel described earlier ceased to have one person for each function (greeting, registering, delivering baggage, etc.) and organized work around the process of getting a guest into the hotel. Likewise, Southwest Airlines organizes its work around the process of getting a flight out on time, as opposed to everyone having a separate and independent function.

Under team management, people are cross-trained around a process so that they can help each other and make the process go more smoothly. In early childhood programs, this might mean blurring the lines among the classifications of receptionists, teachers, teacher aids and even cooks. Rather, everyone would be responsible to receive children in the morning, get to know the parents, help provide the meals, and work together, when time permits, on the different age groups of children. Though there will still be different job descriptions, they would be more flexible. People would be expected to do a variety of tasks depending on the need.

Organizing work around processes has several advantages. First, it reduces goal displacement because the function of each staff member is to make the entire process work. Each staff member perceives that his or her effort represents more than a single cog in a large wheel. They are responsible for the outcome—not just one piece of the work.

When organizations tie this process to the overall cause of the group and show how it relates to the mission, child care professionals also feel more committed to a cause. This promotes team spirit and a sense of ownership because each staff member is responsible for the entire process, not just one station on "an assembly line."

Cooperation and collective decision-making produce positive results for several reasons. First, it gives those affected by decisions some ownership for the outcome of those decisions. If you make a decision for me, it is your decision, and my cooperation will be obtained mainly because of external rewards or punishments. If we make a decision together, however, I have a stake in the outcome—it is also my decision, and I feel ownership for the results.

A second reason cooperation works so well is because it links us together in a unique way. Many experiments have shown that cooperation produces good feelings and more harmonious relationships, while top-down relationships in which one has power over another produce resentment and detachment. We feel a stronger team spirit when we are really a team-not just underlings doing what we are told by management. This makes it possible for all to unite around a common cause.

A third structural characteristic of team management is the introduction of greater informality, or more closeness, in relationships. This change, which correlates with the greater equalization of power, reduces the distance between people. Often, this might mean reducing the use of formal titles. It might also warrant a more relaxed dress code. Formal rules are also commonly reduced, being replaced with basic ground rules that everyone agrees on.

Finally, team management also means that communication becomes less rigid and formal. People are encouraged to communicate with staff in other divisions, without "going through formal channels." In many organizations, the number of social events increases. These are often boisterous celebrations of team success (as opposed to recognizing outstanding individuals), where everyone "let's their hair down" a bit.

The Organizational Culture Needed for Team Management

Earlier, we pointed out that the way people collectively define a situation strongly influences their behavior. The combination of these collective definitions or the shared "mindset," is what we call an organizational culture. With an effective organizational culture, you can get people energized to support the purposes of your organization. This will raise the level of expectations of child care professionals and parents.

On the other hand, a negative organizational culture makes it increasingly necessary to prod, threaten, and rely on external forms of motivation. The organizational culture associated with team management helps people define hard work as something essential. It promotes a willingness to sacrifice for the good of the program. Consequently, everyone benefits.

Creating a truly energizing organizational culture takes a great deal of time and commitment. It will not be accomplished with slogans and lectures. In reality, it will emerge from a set of shared experiences, many of which can be neither planned nor predicted. This is illustrated by the following account described by one agency's grant writer.

When I first started writing grants, I never could get one funded. Once, I was writing a nutrition grant, which had never gotten funded before. Several of us were talking about it, and someone said, "Hey, let's ask the cooks for their suggestions." Well, it got funded! Then we said, "This is how we should do it all the time." Now we never quit or give up. We help each other realize there is always some way to get things done. The lines of authority here have become somewhat blurred, with everyone being responsive to everyone else. I don't supervise, manage, or oversee anyone, but I don't have any trouble getting help for writing grants, or for anything else. Everyone has his or her eye on the goal. We all know what it means for the families that we serve. That is all everyone thinks about when asked to do anything extra. Everyone is willing to stay late, if necessary, to get a short-term project or grant request done.

While much of creating a positive organizational culture like this cannot be planned, you can plot the general direction and get the team to work with you to create it. An organizational culture that really energizes action in positive ways has several key elements. We'll review them and then discuss how team management can be used to help bring them about.

The first element is a deep commitment to the well being of the children in your care. This element was clear in the preceding example described by the grant writer. It may be one of the easiest elements to build in your organizational culture because many early childhood professionals have chosen the field because of their love for children. Still, there are many whose vision has fallen. Another Head Start Program we are familiar with has become so involved in "in-fighting" and "turf-building" that many individuals have lost their vision and their sense of cause. In essence, they have become "brick layers," rather than "temple builders." The team has to find ways to keep this value uppermost in everyone's mind each day.

The second element of your culture is a deep commitment to ever-increasing levels of quality. In essence, you collectively commit yourselves to make each month and each year better than the previous one. You find ways to measure your progress because you are committed to higher and higher standards of quality. This includes the quality of the care given, as well as the quality of relationships with your community and among child care professionals in the program. This is not about being better than some other program. It's about always being better than you were last year, or last month.

A third critical element of organizational culture is its emphasis on teamwork and cooperation. This means you recognize and reward team successes, giving less importance to outstanding individual efforts. As the box 3.1 illustrates, being a team player who brings out the best in others is valued much more than the Lone Ranger who outperforms everyone else.

As we have indicated previously, however, the form of team leadership is a poor substitute for its substance. Simply dressing up boss-style management to look or sound like team leadership creates cynicism, as the following comment by a child care professional in one program illustrates:

> The place where I currently work has a break room lined with posters and graphics, each with catchy phrases designed to improve our motivation. Nevertheless, the child care professionals of this particular workplace have the least energy and motivation of any that I've seen.

Building a culture of team leadership requires a lot more walk than talk. We have to live it so that it becomes a natural part of how we work with each other. Anything else will be seen as manipulation and just another fad.

A big part of building such a culture comes from the **fourth element of desired organizational culture--an emphasis on intrinsic rewards** and a sense of ownership. As we discussed in Chapter 2, child care professionals and parents like to be part of a team. Another intrinsic reward is feeling part of a great cause, in this case being able to really make a difference for disadvantaged children. Ownership is a primary source of intrinsic motivation. The people most affected by decisions are involved in these decisions and are expected to take ownership for solving problems. All of these intrinsic rewards are highly satisfying and encourage people to put in more than a minimal effort.

A fifth element of a strong organizational culture is a

> **Box 3.1**
>
> **A Valuable Lesson**
> During WWII, three young men who grew up together joined the Army. They decided to try out for a very elite unit. Only one man out of every 100 would make it through the training. Because of their religious background, they had maintained a healthy lifestyle and were in excellent physical condition. The young men felt they stood a good chance of being selected, so all enlisted.
> At the end of the first day, they were required to run an endurance course with fully loaded packs. If anyone could not run the distance, they were automatically eliminated. The three young men were pleased to finish first and congratulated each other.
> Upon returning to the barracks, many of the other men avoided them. "Just jealousy," they concluded. After finishing first again the second day, the cold shoulder turned to hostile comments, which got even worse when they finished first again on the third day.
> Finally, one of them asked another man why they were so angry. "You guys are always hotdogging and showing off," he was told. "Some of us could probably beat you guys, but we stay back and try to help others make it too."
> When they also started helping others, they felt a strong sense of unity and acceptance. It really was about more than finishing first.

strong emphasis on quality over quantity. This is not easy to do, especially in programs funded by federal or state agencies. Such agencies commonly insist on numerical data, always in the name of "accountability." We do use numbers to measure progress, but we can never forget that they are only symbols for something much more basic-the quality of care given. So, don't mistake the indicator for the real thing. The quality of care your children receive is much more important than the numbers crunched to prove you are doing a good job. Pay close attention to annual reviews, but refrain from letting them and the data they generate become the real thing. In child care organizations, the real thing is the quality of care provided and the differences made for good in the lives of the people we serve.

How to Create a Positive Organizational Culture

Creating an organization with the cultural elements just described is not easy. It will not happen with a few meetings or admonitions. Most organizations have to work intensely at it over extended periods of time, sometimes for several years. But, just as small ships can change direction faster than large ones, smaller organizations can bring about cultural and structural change more quickly than large ones. It is important that everyone recognize this will not be a quick fix. The following strategies will help you make your organizational culture a powerful force for good.

1. Recognize that a substantial and a sustained effort will be required. Changing the way people collectively think is a major change that takes time. The most important aspect of a sustained effort will be to get a firm vision of where you want to go and what you (collectively) want to become. Though we will discuss this in greater detail in Chapter Five, we can say here that you must constantly help people sense the importance of what they are doing. Change may be rough. People need to remind each other why the change is worthwhile. In essence, you must not only map out for each other a firm idea of where you are going, but you must also constantly validate the journey—showing why dedicated efforts will be worth it.

Stick with basics. Find out what changes are the most important and stick with them. Remember—the main thing is to keep the main thing the main thing. Get everyone, especially yourself, to walk the talk. Stay on message. People need to know that what you are leading them toward is not a passing fad. Approach it from different angles, but keep it always as your main focus.

2. Watch for and be ready to deal with opposition. Every organization will experience some opposition to change, especially when the change involves all that is required for true team management. You can anticipate several potential sources of opposition. People with power may not want to relinquish control. Conversely, those accustomed to following orders might resist having to be more responsible. Child care professionals who are comfortable with the way things are may fear change and the adjustments it will require. Others may be weary of "fads" and hope to wait this change out, thinking it's just a passing fancy. Watch for opposition, but don't become confrontational. Listen to those who have reservations. Really listen. Then, do whatever can legitimately be done to address their concerns. Help them to recognize that what you are seeking to do addresses many of their needs. Involve them in making changes in areas where they are willing to make it happen.

As team management is seriously implemented, people will come to enjoy feeling ownership for the work they do, regardless of their previous attitudes. Those who want to be taken seriously (probably all of us) will feel empowered and recognize that they are increasingly taken into account. Build a coalition that is always seeking to attract—not isolate-

those who might oppose you. The sense of group unity will attract others, as will the powerful sense of cause that develops out of some group sessions you will hold. In short, with patience and perseverance, team leadership will help overcome most resistance to this important change.

3. Make it fun. As you seek to develop the appropriate culture with team management, make it enjoyable and fun. Nothing binds a group together better than some outstanding enjoyment that is clearly related to its mutual cause and goals. Many organizations that use team management mix in a great deal of fun. Sam Walton, founder of Wal-Mart, used this principle to make his company the world's leading retailer. He loved to use intense "rah-rah and hokum" to build enthusiasm. He stated:

> Just because we work so hard, we don't have to go around with long faces all the time, taking ourselves seriously, pretending that we're lost in thought over weighty problems...While we're doing this work, we like to have a good time...We not only have a heck of a good time with it, we work better because of it. We build spirit and excitement. We break down barriers, which helps us communicate better with one another. And we make our people feel part of a family in which no one is too important or too puffed up to lead a cheer or be the butt of a joke-or the target of a persimmon-seed spitting contest...We know that our antics-our company cheer or our songs or my hula-can sometimes be pretty corny, or hokey. We couldn't care less.[6]

Likewise, Herb Kelleher of Southwest Airlines uses a keen sense of humor in very lively celebrations of team success. While there will always be many serious moments, team management uses humor and enthusiasm to build excitement and help everyone truly enjoy each other. These fun moments become legends that give people stories to tell and re-tell. They are an important way to build team culture. One early childhood agency has made having fun an important part of their culture. They say:

> How do we make it fun? We eat a lot. We get together once a month and bring food and just gather and talk. Last week, one of the departments made lunch for everyone just out of the blue. Another department is going to decorate the office for Halloween. They thought it would be fun. We also go places together, and we will get together socially. Sometimes, we even go out of town for concerts.

4. Avoid manipulation. At all costs, avoid manipulation. Nothing will turn people against you faster than to find they have been manipulated into supporting something. Do not hold team meetings, for example, to come to a "decision" that you have already made. Similarly, you must "walk the talk." You cannot talk of a great cause to others and yet not believe fiercely in it yourself. If you send others on a journey you are not willing to take yourself, it will ring hollow and people will not follow. Building a powerful culture in your organization requires a great deal of trust. You are asking people not simply for compliance, but for a deeper commitment. You need them not only to change their behavior, but also to fundamentally transform their way of thinking. Manipulation will destroy the trust needed to build these things, so *never* use it.

5. Avoid relying on slogans. If you use slogans at all, be sure that they stand for something that is real. If you use them, make sure that they come from a total team effort, as a symbol of a commitment already made and deeply felt. Otherwise, they will be seen as a manipulation by management and will be ridiculed or resisted.

6. Put principles over programs. Principles are general guides to action based on truths about human behavior. Programs, on the other hand, are highly controlled efforts designed for short-term or quick results. In essence, following programs is like painting by numbers and connecting dots. Following principles is like painting by inspiration. People get tired of new programs. They learn to wait for each to pass as just another fad. If you base your program on principles, they will be part of your culture and will serve as long-term guides for the behavior of everyone.

7. Put your highest priority on building and maintaining trust. If you constantly look for the good in people and have high expectations, you communicate trust. Indeed, you will not be able to empower child care professionals unless you see something in them that allows you to trust them to make important decisions. There will be times when this is difficult. But as you truly empower members of the team, they will reciprocate with ownership and commitment.

8. Teach people under your direction that it's safe to take calculated risks. One of the pioneers of Team Management, E. Edwards Deming urged leaders to drive out fear. People will not be willing to seek better ways to meet team goals if they fear punishment and ridicule for expressing ideas. You must also let them learn from mistakes without being punished for them. Indeed, if you are willing to use intrinsic motivation, fear will become less important because you stop using punishment to accomplish team purposes.

In subsequent chapters we will return to many of these points. They are introduced here to illustrate the importance of the type of team culture you are trying to build. As people begin to define situations in these ways, they will become real in their consequences. You will truly have an organization that values and promotes excellence.

Chapter Application Exercises
A. Personal Reflection Exercise: Which Type of Leadership?
In the personal reflection exercise in Chapter Two, we had you reflect on the level of readiness of people under your direction for additional responsibility. In this chapter, we suggest that you reflect on how their level of readiness should correspond with your type of leadership. Please

refer to the figure entitled, "Appropriate Leadership Roles, in Reference to Development Levels of Those You Supervise," presented earlier in the chapter, Figure 3.1. As you do so, reflect on different individuals in your organization who might need each type of assistance. Then, ask yourself if you are prepared to give the appropriate help to each individual. What additional learning do you need to be able to accomplish this?

B. Group Exercise: A Cultural Analysis of Your Organization

Probably the most important impact of culture in any organization, for good or for bad, comes from that portion which is unspoken, but widely shared. Each organization, for example, has a lot of "unwritten rules." One organization that analyzed their "unwritten culture" found that almost everyone felt it was okay to have a meeting without an agenda and without clear expectations for positive outcomes. They also found that, while everyone was expected to come to meetings, it was not a bad thing to come unprepared. They also found that people who didn't perform well were allowed to slide by because no one wanted to be hard on their friends. Finally, they found that many people were not expected to be involved in decisions and were not being held accountable for results.

The best clue for this hidden culture is behavior. Most of us pay lip service to a lot of ideals or standards, but behave quite differently. Groups, working together, can frequently see through their organization's "hidden culture." Help your people understand that when they behave contrary to group standards, they are, in effect, changing the culture. In effect, their behavior tells everyone that those standards are really not very important.

Each person should take some time, working alone, to try and identify elements of hidden culture that are counter to the culture you all really want to have. After each person has had this opportunity, get together to determine what your organizational culture really is. Be sure to identify both the positive aspects that people really do believe in, as well as those that get only lip service, and little behavioral support.

You may want to use the following questions to suggest some areas of your group's culture.

1. How do you feel about the use of time? How often do you make each other wait? In what ways are meetings often wasteful of time?
2. Would you say that people in your organization are more cooperative or more competitive? Do most people enjoy seeing someone else succeed, or do they feel that someone else's win represents a loss for them?
3. How honest are you with each other? Can you give negative, as well as positive, feedback? Can you be honest without rubbing it in or being hurtful? If you give someone honest feedback that is unpleasant, do you do things afterwards to show them increased respect and sincere friendship?

4. How do you really feel about the community you serve? Do you make snide remarks or complain a lot about its failings? Do you truly see the good in the community and have high expectations for better behavior?
5. How high are your standards for: Quality in teaching? Care-giving? Service to your community? Cleanliness? For involving parents in the operation of your program? Do you collectively want to exceed the standards of your funding agency, or just get the numbers they are looking for?

Chapter Notes

---

1. Based on Maureen Down, *The New York Times*, March 12, 1984, B1.

2. Adapted from Bibb Lanane and John M. Darley, *The Unresponsive Bystander* (New York: Apleton, Century, Frofts, 1970.

3. Stanley Milgram, *Obedience to Authority* (New York: Harper, 1974).

4. Carol Tavris, *Anger: The Misunderstood Emotion* (New York: Simon and Schuster, 1982), 87, 88.

5. We base much of the following discussion about situational leadership on Duncan and Pinegar.

6. Summarized from Sam Walton and John Huey, *Sam Walton: Made in America* (New York: Doubleday, 1992), 156-159.

Chapter 4.
"The Whole is Greater than the Sum of Its Parts."
Empowering Your Team.

Chapter Summary

This chapter describes how to form effective teams, what decisions they should be empowered to make, and how to make them accountable for results. Additionally, it presents many of the skills (structured creativity, problem solving, consensus building and holding effective meetings) that team leaders need in order to help their teams produce outstanding results.

Introduction

Our director used to be a school principal. When he came to our agency, he talked a lot about "team spirit." He also used to lecture us about "being team players." He thought that was team management. But his style of management was anything but team management. Being a "team player" meant you did what he told you to do. And "team spirit" was being enthusiastic about his decisions. To make matters worse, he not only wanted to make all the decisions, but he would then try to oversee every detail in how we implemented them. As a result, nobody wanted to take initiative for anything. And he couldn't figure out why we had none of his "team spirit".

Like this supervisor, many early childhood leaders have experienced boss-style management disguised as team management. Managers who pick only the language or the trappings of team management have little desire to share authority with others. Some try to be more inclusive but return to their old ways when immediate success is not achieved. Others make serious commitments to principles of inclusion only to find that team meetings turn into gripe sessions or seemingly endless debates, so they go back to their old ways.

Team management is about more than team meetings. Teams have to be empowered to solve problems. If you're the problem-solver of your organization, you should not be surprised if no one else is as concerned about the overall well-being of your organization as you are. It takes time and patience to truly implement team leadership, despite the occasional setbacks. You should not allow this to discourage you. Developing effective teams will pay rich dividends far into the future. They are worth the effort.

How Trust is Related to Ownership

For many leaders, the hardest part of team management is learning to really trust "subordinates." Trust is essential in creating an environment of ownership and an indispensable part of team management. You cannot keep inspecting their work and revising their decisions without destroying the sense of ownership of results (as the box story at right illustrates, 4.1).

Trust is a very high compliment. It brings out the best in people. But you cannot fully trust your people unless you have searched diligently for the good in them. This is the power of positive expectations described in Chapter Two. When trust is sincere, it helps others assume ownership for solving problems and getting results.

This does not mean you need to be gullible. There are, of course, some people who have not reached the level at which we can deposit full trust in them. Sometimes, we find trust difficult because integrity is lacking. Other times, it is because skill has

---

Box 4.1

A Tough Decision

An Air Force general, up for promotion, was scheduled for a major inspection flight. The procedure, under the inspection of another officer, would require that he thoroughly inspect the work of the maintenance crew on his aircraft before making the flight.

This posed a problem. His crew knew that he trusted them completely and had always refused to inspect their work. As he and his senior officer approached the plane, he could see the crew was watching. They also knew that an inspection of their work was required, but wanted to see what he would do.

"I decided to lose some points on the inspection," he said, "rather than let them think I did not trust them. It was worth it. Within hours, word had spread among all the maintenance crews. From then on, my plane was the best-maintained aircraft on base. They would never betray that kind of trust."

not been sufficiently developed. Whatever the case may be, without placing trust in your people, you will never empower them to take ownership for results.

In his book *Principle-Centered Leadership*, Stephen R. Covey[1] proposes that trust is an emotional bank account between people. We work hard to build the account on both ends. This suggests that you need to give people many opportunities to increase your trust in them. It also means that you should try hard to notice what they do well so that you can trust them.

A high level of trust improves communication, facilitates empowerment, and helps people accept ownership. Trust motivates people to realize their potential, helps them be more innovative, and allows them to assume responsibility for their own behavior. In addition, trust creates win-win situations rather than those where one person wins only if another loses.

So how do you build this kind of trust? Start with yourself. Be trustworthy. Avoid making promises you will fail to keep. Never betray confidences. Do not manipulate people. You cannot speak convincingly of empowerment and trust if you then continue to practice control and close monitoring. Pay the price. Be a person of integrity.

You can also change how you react to others. Covey recommends that we react to someone who is hard to trust "... .with the eye of faith and treat him in terms of his potential, not his behavior. . . . This isn't to say that we trust him unconditionally, but it does mean that we treat him respectfully and trust him conditionally".[2] We search for the good in him and focus less and less on his failings. It is like seeing someone who has a spill on her blouse. Do we focus more on the spot, or on the otherwise clean blouse? We have to make the strengths of others our primary focus, not their "spots."

Goethe says in this regard, "Treat a man as he is, and he will remain as he is; treat a man as he can and should be, and he will become as he can and should be." We feel a powerful enticement to improve when someone expects something great of us. Often, this is because they see things in us that we do not even see in ourselves. This requires an ability to look beyond present weaknesses to potential strengths. They then hold up this image that reflects our strong points.

A classic experiment in the public school setting demonstrated this point a number of years ago. Two researchers, Rosenthall and Jacobsen[3], told first- and second-grade teachers that a standardized test had predicted certain children would be "spurting" or "blooming" during the year. In reality, the alleged "spurters" and "bloomers" were randomly given these labels without any justification from the test. At the end of the year, these positively-labeled students had made significant IQ gains over other children. The gains were greatest for minority children.

Rosenthal and Jacobson concluded that when teachers have positive expectations of children, the children live up to those expectations.

It is not always easy to trust those with whom we work, or to maintain high expectations of them in light of less-than-superior performance. We do so by giving them increasing authority to accept and solve difficult problems. Often, you must honor their decisions even if yours might be better. You do it because you want to build trust and transfer ownership. You must learn to let go and get others to assume ownership for problems and for finding solutions.

This does not mean you should turn all decisions over to your team. Some decisions you should make yourself. Some teams operate on the rule that calls for top management to decide what will be done, but lets team members determine how the decision will be carried out. Even greater teamwork is called for by another rule-one which states that if you need: **(1) their knowledge; (2) their cooperation; or (3) their commitment, they should be involved in the decision and its implementation.** Let's examine the three elements of this last rule a bit more closely.

It is generally true that those closest to the action have the best knowledge of what is happening. Teachers, for example, will know the most about the children in your center and their special needs. Home-based visitors will likely be the best informed about parents and the tough situations they face. The cooks will be most acquainted with the problems of food preparation (remember the grant writer who got a nutrition grant after she consulted the cooks?). Even your secretary or receptionist will have a great deal of information and knowledge that you lack.

If this knowledge will help produce a better decision, then involve those possessing it. When they really feel ownership, they will not only identify problems but will propose solutions. Indeed, when you truly empower them, they will identify problems, work with you to create solutions, and keep you informed about what they are doing. Thus, you cease to be the "fix-it" person and become a facilitator for the team members as they own and fix problems.

Ownership is the biggest part of this equation. Even if you could devise a better solution than your team (say, for example, your solution scores a "10" and theirs is only a "7") it would often be better to go with their solution. That's because they would keep working to make theirs work, while they would have little ownership in making your solution succeed. This is suggested in the following case.

> A cook in one center was always calling in sick, sometimes up to three days a week. This caused a chain reaction of problems. The director had to cover for her, thus spending most of her day in the kitchen. As a result, she got little work done, and teachers and child care professional were unavailable to work with the children and families. They all spent a lot of time working out ways to "cover"

for the cook's absences. On days she failed to come in, everyone had short tempers.

For a long time, no one would talk with the cook about it, believing the director needed to "fix" the problem herself. Indeed, she had tried--many times, but with little success. Finally, at a child care professional meeting, with the help of a facilitator and when the cook was present, the child care professional began to talk about what they ALL could do when the cook was out. They suggested that she cook extra food and freeze it so that when she was gone, they would only have to heat up the food. They talked about systems of delivering the food to the rooms and cleaning the dishes and the kitchen during nap times or after the children left. They asked her for suggestions on how to do these various things from her perspective. She was very surprised and actually pleased that they were asking her about her work. She also expressed a feeling of value. She did not realize how much she mattered to the center's daily operation. She offered many suggestions and together, they worked out a system of cooking while she was out.

To their surprise, however, she was rarely absent after that meeting. She made arrangements to not be gone during the times of cooking and cleaning. She re-arranged her appointments and became much more involved in the center's operation as a whole. Before, she had never been a part of the team and felt isolated. Her change in behavior came about as she felt included and valued.

While involving child care professionals in decisions is important from a motivational perspective, it has other benefits. One is how responsive it makes your organization. The airline industry estimates that when most catastrophes occur, someone has already spotted the problem but failed to communicate it. "It wasn't my job" is the common excuse. You need your child care professional's eyes and ears to spot problems before they become major crises.

But, do not settle for just their eyes and ears. Get their hearts and their minds involved as well. If you empower them and give them ownership, they will increasingly **cooperate** to produce a solution at least as good as what you might have devised and then find ways to make it work. Many decisions fail because people fail to cooperate. Often, their lack of cooperation is not obvious. Some people will go along with a decision, but will fail to take ownership to make sure that it works. Others will use their creativity to find more problems in the new program than you can possibly resolve. A few might even find ways to sabotage your decision.

Cooperation is important, but it is not enough. For a decision to be successful, most child care professionals must also be **committed** to making it succeed. Kurt Lewin,[4] a pioneer social psychologist, demonstrated the relation of group decision-making to commitment. He found that during the food rationing days of World War II, people were much more likely to alter their eating habits if they were involved in discussions and decisions regarding the need to change such behavior. He compared groups that made joint decisions with ones that received only lectures about the need for such changes. He found that people who were asked to participate in making decisions about what to do were *ten times* more likely to accept the changes.

To repeat, if you need the knowledge, the cooperation, or the commitment of people affected by a decision, it is wise to involve them as much as possible in making the decision. You must frequently weigh these three elements against other factors, however. Occasionally, confidentiality will keep you from fully involving others. In other cases, there may not be time to go through the group decision-making process. In such cases, ask for their trust. They will be more likely to give it if they know that you *do* involve them whenever you can.

Other Principles of Transferring Ownership

In order to transfer ownership, you must increasingly empower your people. This becomes easier to do as you build an organizational culture in which **cooperation** and **excellence** are valued by everyone. As we pointed out in Chapter Three, people must come to enjoy cooperating with each other and see that results of doing so are much greater than could be achieved by the aspiring "hot dog." In addition, they must identify steady improvement and excellence as strongly-held ideals of the group.

This group mindset also encourages a certain amount of **risk-taking**. Everyone needs to know that it is safe to be innovative. Unfortunately, because people want some degree of safety and security, organizations often discourage them from taking necessary risks. Ships are safe in a harbor, but that's not what ships are for. Similarly, people need to venture increasingly farther from the safety of comfort zones. You will find much satisfaction in helping someone get out of the harbor to discover what their true capabilities are.

To do so, they will need to know that your organization allows for making honest mistakes as an expected part of learning. If this really is the climate you create, people will be much more willing to accept ownership. Otherwise, they will play it safe avoiding responsibility and blame by refusing to take any risks.

David Langford[5] relates a story that serves to illustrate the importance of considering the making of mistakes an important step toward improving performance.

> Let's put failure in its right place. Only in schools do we think of failure as bad. When my son learned to walk, we knew he was ready. We stood him up-my wife over there and me here. We were cheering. We knew he could do it. We let him go and, sure enough, he took three steps and fell right on his face. So what did we do?

Picked him up, hugged him, and set him up again? No, we gave him an "F" and sent him to two years of remedial walking school. Seriously, that's what we do in schools daily across the country.

Of course, schools are not the only organizations in which people are made to fear taking chances. How do you change this mentality in your organization? Start by asking yourself how you handle the mistakes of others. If you criticize, blame, or punish, you will stifle risk-taking, and no one will want to accept ownership. If, on the other hand, a child care professional made a mistake because she took the initiative to solve a problem, then recognize and reward her initiative and help her see what she could have done better.

If mistakes happen because someone is self-centered, thoughtless, or grossly careless, you may need to discipline him. Remember, though, that there is an important difference between discipline and punishment. Punishment is what you do *to* someone, but discipline is what you do *for* them. You are not trying to control their behavior. You use discipline when attempting to get them to accept ownership for doing something truly worthwhile. Where possible, try to let natural consequences rather than contrived punishments, discipline poor decisions.

Be careful, however, never to discipline a team member in front of the team. Humiliation and embarrassment are very poor motivators. People will go to great lengths to avoid public reprimands. Forcing this shame on someone creates resentment and produces far more negative side effects than you can handle. The practice also creates a climate of fear that discourages people from taking risks. As box 4.2 suggests, it is far better to catch people doing something right and recognize it than it is to punish their "bad" behavior.

Indeed, the best correction will often come from fellow team members. Staff members who would resist correction from a manager often accept it when it represents the collective

---

Box 4.2

What Animals Can Teach Us

A few years ago, my wife and I were taking her parents through the San Diego Zoo. The bus we were on would stop in front of each animal display, and the driver would call out for the animals to perform some trick. When we got to the bears, for example, he would call one of them by name and ask him to wave. He'd ask another to roll over or perform some other impressive feat, always with positive results.

Thoroughly impressed, I took the driver aside at the end of the tour and asked who had trained the animals. With evident pride, he responded, "We did—us—the bus drivers."

When asked how he knew so much about animal training, he replied, "It's simple. We just watch for them to do something we like and reward it."

will of a valued team. This is one of the reasons why a positive team culture is important. Team members support the values and standards that are firmly rooted in their collective culture or mindset.

As this team culture emerges and team members accept increasing ownership of results, the nature of your job will change. Rather than directing the actions of others, you will support, train, and facilitate. You will also help the team maintain a focus on its primary mission. You will help them identify goals that flow from this mission and that work together to formulate specific plans to carry them out (more on this in Chapter Five). You will use meetings to have your team monitor its progress toward these goals by focusing on a few factors that are evidence of a great performance. Finally, as the leader, you will work with outside organizations (or higher administration) to clear obstacles that might block the success of your team.

Specific Team Leadership Skills

While the preceding principles are important, they cannot be accomplished without learning some basic team management skills. These skills include structured brainstorming, consensus building, problem solving, effective team meetings, and summarizing/checking for understanding. We will present basic concepts here, then provide some exercises to use with your team so that you can become proficient in their use.

Structured Brainstorming.

It's difficult to find anyone who has not had an experience with brainstorming. Unfortunately, the experience was not positive for many. In some cases, a few outspoken people dominated the discussion. At other times, people could not resist the temptation to criticize ideas as soon as they were mentioned. As a result, brainstorming has its critics, and many who have had such experiences are turned off by it.

Guess what. The critics are right! Experiments on decision-making show that letting individuals work alone, then pooling their ideas, produces more creativity than does letting the same number of people go at it in a regular brainstorming session. In one study by the 3M Corporation, the approach of pooling individual responses generated 30 percent more ideas than did ordinary group brainstorming.[6]

The problem lies in the unstructured nature of most brainstorming sessions. When brainstorming is structured in some fairly simple ways, it can be 100 percent more effective in producing good ideas than in an unstructured format. Structured brainstorming combines the best elements of the individual and the group approaches. One director who has used it comments:

> I have tried really hard to move our program directors towards this style of management. I insist, for example, that they come prepared to help make decisions, so I expect them to read the material I

give them beforehand. They cannot expect to come to the meeting and be read to. This allows us to spend time on real issues. At the last meeting, we worked in small groups brainstorming new communication techniques for our agency. We created lists and then came together to combine or refine our lists. Then, we looked at which person would have to do what to make it work. Participation has skyrocketed since we began expecting everyone to participate. Now, they realize that they are there to help make the decisions, so they have to speak up.

The **first** rule of structured brainstorming is to use a facilitator who is respected by participants. This person could be a manager or just a respected team member. She should manage the process, but not the outcome. In other words, the facilitator keeps the group moving toward a decision, but lets it come from the group. Make sure you have a facilitator who can resist trying to control the outcome. Her assignment to manage only the process is very important.

A **second** rule is to give each individual adequate time to prepare. The facilitator presents the problem or issue to group members several days before the meeting and asks them to write down several suggestions to bring to the session. It is important that the issue be clearly stated, in written form, so that all who participate understand essentially what ideas are needed.

Third, maximize participation. Everyone will be expected to present at least one idea. The facilitator may proceed in a round-robin fashion, or take ideas as they are volunteered. When selecting the volunteer approach, the facilitator should keep track of who has not participated and ask them to share at least one idea. The round-robin approach works best when working with individuals who tend to dominate discussions. The facilitator may need to limit suggestions from these few until everyone has had a turn.

Fourth, hold off criticisms or evaluating comments until all ideas are on the table. This is not easy to do. Inevitably, someone will say something like, "We've already tried that, and it didn't work." The facilitator will have to be firm in holding off critical comments. People need to feel free to bring up creative suggestions. In fact, it is often helpful to tell everyone to present at least one "wild" idea just to encourage creativity. The facilitator could ask people to keep from being critical of their own ideas. Remember, at this stage you do not want to censor thoughts-even your own.

Finally, select the best ideas. This may involve examining which ideas are essentially the same, or those which might be combined in a meaningful way. The facilitator may want to break the team up into "subcommittees" or keep everyone together. In either case, the ideas should be written where everyone can see them. The team then tries to gain consensus on the best ideas.

One technique that might break a logjam is to give each team member a set number of points to "spend" on the ideas listed. Each person should be able to spend at least two points, though the ideal number of points everyone can "spend" would be about one-fourth of the total number of ideas to be evaluated. If someone feels very strongly about one idea, she could spend all her points on that one. Or, the points could be distributed among several ideas. A tally is then made to see which ideas scored the greatest number of points. Do not stop there, however. The group must then reach a consensus on which ideas everyone will support.

Problem Solving.

One area in which structured creativity works very well is in problem solving. Every organization confronts problems on a daily basis. Often, people who work in organizations see problem-solving as something the "boss" should do. This way of thinking is risky, as the following story illustrates.

> **Corporate Executive:** I was a world-class rescuer. I was owning all the responsibility for fixing problems. Their job was to identify what needed to be fixed, and they were truly dedicated to doing that job well. My "fix them" leadership paradigm was failing.
>
> Early in my leadership career, I had read about employee involvement. It sounded good, so I began holding employee meetings to get participation. These rapidly deteriorated, however, into bitch sessions. They kept bringing up situations that needed "fixing."
>
> So, I called a meeting and asked them for their input on fixing it. This time, however, I insisted that they had to be responsible for implementing any solution they suggested. The discussion took a very different tack. Their first suggestion was to change equipment. When I said that would cost $1.5million, they were shocked. Next, they suggested that I talk the customer into taking a lesser quality product. I arranged for a group of them to meet with the customer and discuss it face-to-face with him. They returned with higher quality standards, not lower ones. One of the group told me, "This is hard work!"
>
> I realized that I had trained them to be dependent upon me. I asked them if they would rather I made the decision. They mumbled something about "Well...no. But it isn't supposed to be so hard." After what seemed like an eternity (it was only four days), they came back with a plan to redo several of the procedures and learn a new process. Total cost: less than $10,000. And it solved the quality problem. "Go for it," I said. It took maximum control for me to keep from reading their proposal and "improving" it. My restraint paid big dividends. The execution of their own plan was flawless. The problem was solved and never came back. Gradually, I learned to transfer responsibility for solving problems to the rightful owner.[7]

As long as this boss was willing to "fix" problems, his employees became very good at finding them. Indeed, they could find more problems than he could solve. In addition, they felt no ownership for making his solutions work. They were his solutions. When he made the team responsible for problem solving, they took ownership not only for finding a solution, but also for making it work within the constraints of time, money, and increased quality.

As this case illustrates, the transition was difficult not only for the boss but also for his employees. He had to give up some of his authority and change his idea of what a good boss does. The employees, on the other hand, had to be willing to take ownership for finding solutions and making them work. This was also true in the following case.

> When people come to me with a problem or a dilemma, I usually give it back to them as a question. They have to learn to figure things out for themselves. Some people like that, but it frustrates others. Many staff members want me to make the decision, but I won't do it. At first, they thought I was being indecisive. I kept asking them questions, trying to help them think through a decision.
>
> One time, for example, the teachers wanted to bring their children to our evening meetings with parents. Some directors thought it was unfair to provide "free babysitting." Others thought we might run into liability issues. I told them it should be a site-based decision. But they insisted on a uniform, agency-wide policy. So, I went along and made a rule that no one could bring their kids.
>
> There were immediate protests. Some teachers could not leave their children at home. One decision just did not fit all the centers. So, we went back to look at it again. We talked to our attorneys and asked about liability again. After looking more closely, they determined that we were covered. So we talked about it again. After each director talked to their own staff, they each came up with a policy that worked best for them.

Though it may be just as difficult for center and program directors to trust their employees as it has been for business leaders, we can offer some suggestions that may make the transition less painful. First, consider the type of problems they can be given as they learn problem-solving skills. It is generally best not to start with relationship problems. Relationship difficulties are often accompanied by intense feelings and may result in conflict that your team is not yet ready to handle. Instead, let them work on problems that stand in the way of accomplishing important work goals. If they are just learning problem-solving skills, give them problems that they can solve themselves without having to go to higher-ups for permission or additional resources to implement solutions.

Suppose, for example, that several of your staff members habitually come to work late. This creates delays for everyone and disrupts the process of welcoming children and getting needed information from their parents. Some staff attempt to compensate for other staff members' late arrival, but their own work is made more difficult by having to do someone else's job. This is certainly a problem that requires the knowledge, the cooperation, and the commitment of all the staff members. Relinquish the problem to them to solve and assure them you will do all you can to support any decision on which they can agree.

Second, we suggest you encourage employees to tackle problems whose mastery will allow them to be the heroes. Like the boss in the preceding story, you must resist the temptation to approve everything, or try to improve on what your employees do. If you want them to take ownership, be willing to forego always having the final say or putting on the finishing touches. Try to live with any decisions they make. If what they are suggesting is too expensive or would cause problems for you in the future, inform them of these constraints along with the problem and ask for solutions to overcome these obstacles.

Our third suggestion is for you to teach your team to use a structured approach to problem solving. A considerable body of research has shown that an organized or structured approach produces more effective solutions than informal methods. While there are many models, we suggest one along the lines of that proposed by Dennis Romig.[8]

The first step is to identify and clarify the problem. Using our example about late arrivals, ask your team to determine how this problem is keeping them from meeting their most important goals. Also, suggest that they ask each other if they have accurate and reliable information about the problem. Have them find out what they don't know and determine if such information is obtainable. The more specific team members can become in describing problems, the better will be their solutions. Have them detail who is experiencing the problem, when it usually occurs, and what effects it is producing. At this stage, do not allow team members to engage in fault-finding.

A second step is to accurately determine the effects of this problem. What is it costing your organization? What side effects is it creating (both positive and negative)? How great is the cost to your organization and to the families you serve?

In the third step, that of finding probable causes, avoid finger pointing. Here the question is more "What is to blame?" than it is "Who is to blame?" Don't let your child care professional be sidelined with superficial causes. It is important to get at the more basic reasons. You do this by asking "why?" to superficial causes. This helps you focus on root causes, rather than just looking at symptoms. Try to determine which are which.

Let's illustrate using the problem of tardy staff members. Someone might propose that the cause of their chronic tardiness is inadequate commitment to the program. So ask, "What's keeping them from being more committed?" Determine whether the lack of commitment is the problem, or instead, if it is a symptom of something deeper. Make sure that someone is writing down the basic causes so that you can get the team to determine which reasons appear to be most important.

The fourth step is to use the structured creativity process described earlier to brainstorm possible solutions. Give individuals time to write down their own proposed solutions first, then have each individual share them one at a time (with someone writing these down so all can see). Use this process to get the group to suggest many possible solutions, with no one allowed (yet) to criticize anyone else's suggestions.

The fifth step is to evaluate proposed solutions and select the best ones. Initially, this is done by seeing which proposed solutions can be combined and eliminated. Then, ask participants to discuss the pros and cons of the remaining solutions. At this point, you might also want to consider possible "side effects" of any solution you propose. Next, have participants rank the solutions. You may choose to use the point system proposed earlier (giving each person a set number of points they can "spend" on their preferred solutions).

The sixth and final stage of this process is to plan, implement, and evaluate (at a later date) the selected solutions. This is the most important stage. The team must now take **action** to implement its solutions. Discussion at this stage will center on who will do what, by when, and with what resources. Be certain that everyone will actively support the plan. Set up a process to let the team monitor the effects and evaluate the progress of their efforts to implement their solutions.

C o n s e n s u s Building. Consensus is at the very heart of team management. It produces wise decisions and ownership for putting these ideas into practice. Consensus, however, does not

Box 4.3

The Danger of Going Along to Get Along
Business consultant Jerry B. Harvey describes a frustrating visit to his Texas in-laws one summer. Someone suggested driving to Abilene to get something to eat. Everyone went along with the idea. However, after a 106 mile round trip in brutal heat, a dust storm, and a car without air conditioning, all were exhausted. When someone mentioned how bad an idea it had been, each confessed to having not wanted to go in the first place. Harvey calls the tendency for teams to undertake activities that no one really wants "the Abilene Paradox." He says that the inability to manage agreement is more serious than the inability to manage conflict. It happens when team members fail to express desires or beliefs that may seem at odds with the group just to achieve consensus.

require everyone to be wildly enthusiastic about a decision. This seldom happens. Neither does it mean that people should reluctantly go along (as the box 4.3 suggests).[9] Consensus is reached when everyone agrees that they can live with, and even support, a decision. It is not easy to accomplish, but it is worth the effort and the patience it takes to achieve.

In order for a team to reach consensus, hierarchy essentially has to disappear. This means that leaders become team members. George Washington understood this principle well. While presiding over the Constitutional Convention, he would occupy a position on a raised stand while facilitating the discussion. When he wanted to put forth an idea, however, he would ask someone to take his place while he came down from the stand and took a seat at the same level as other participants. By so doing, he was stepping out of his role as the leader to become one among equals.

This requires considerable integrity on the part of a leader. Leaders cannot come to the meeting asking for team members to make a decision that has already been made. They will sense that they are being manipulated and will not take ownership for the decision. If it is a decision that must be made by the leader alone, she must be honest with her team and seek their understanding and support. They must be involved in the decisions that they can really make. It is not worth the risk of losing trust and team ownership to pretend otherwise.

Reaching consensus is a process that people must learn to follow. The members of a team need training on how to achieve it. A group has not reached consensus if someone leaves the meeting and confides to someone else, "Well, that will never work." The team must keep working until every member can support the group decision in public and in private. The exercises at the end of this chapter will allow your team to learn the process while making some important decisions.

Summarizing/Checking for Understanding. A number of other skills are involved in moving toward consensus. One of these is learning to **summarize**. It is most useful when you seem to be at an impasse or when two or more team members are angry or have ceased listening to one another. Essentially, the facilitator calls a "time out," asks each of them to summarize what the other is saying, and gives the other participant a chance to confirm or modify this statement of understanding. This not only calms strong feelings, it gets people to listen more carefully to what others are saying.

Another use of summarizing occurs when the facilitator believes the discussion of a particular point has continued long enough. He or she may then use a request to summarize as a way to move on. This involves asking any team member to summarize the main points of what has been said and allows the team to see where they are before moving on. After summarization, the team may modify the summary to make sure that important points are agreed upon.

A similar skill that must be learned is to **check understanding**. Often, this is something that team members can do without waiting for the intervention of the facilitator. It begins with a statement such as, "Let me see if I understand what you are saying," followed by a concise summary of the main points made by the other person. The individual who checks for understanding may even say that he or she does not agree with what the other is saying, but wants to be sure he or she understands it. In addition to its value in clarifying what someone is saying, checking for understanding also communicates respect for team members, even when we strongly disagree with another's position.

Holding Effective Team Meetings. Meetings are where most team decisions are made. They help produce ownership and allow a team to really unite. Good meetings help fill all sorts of individual needs, such as the desire to be creative or wanting to feel supported by others. Effective meetings also fill important organizational needs, including improved communication, increased cooperation, and better coordination of work. Still, many of us see meetings as places where minutes are taken and hours are wasted.[10] One director, for example, comments:

> I find it very frustrating when there is no agenda, and it is just a free for all. I have to go into it not thinking that I will not get any information or decisions from this. So now when I have a meeting, we have an agenda, prior to the meeting. I go down the agenda, item by item. I try to go down it fairly efficiently, then we go around the table and tell what we have done throughout the past week. This gives the child care professional the opportunity to hear what everyone is doing and how hard everyone is working.

As most of us know, meetings can either drive us to action--or to complete distraction. Knowing how to make meetings really work is an important skill, so let's discuss some of the essential ingredients of a good meeting.

First, frequent, short meetings are better than long, infrequent ones. Short meetings, held on a frequent basis, send the message that each team member's time is important and that their participation is valued. Some meetings, of course, may need to be longer, such as those used to set goals or solve important problems. In such cases, make sure that everyone knows how long the meeting will last and the importance of work to be done.

Second, structured participation should occur early in the meeting. It is a team event so we should not wait too long to let people interact as a team. In fact, some studies suggest that you should not wait longer than fifteen minutes to give people the chance to have structured discussion.[11] Structured discussion has a clear purpose and follows certain ground rules that the team itself agrees upon (more about this in the exercise at the end of the chapter). It is action-oriented--more than just talk. It leads people to solve problems-not just talk about them. Such discussion brings the team together in heart and mind, as well as puts them in the same room.

To accomplish this, resist the temptation to schedule a lot of one-way communication at the front of the meeting. For example, schedule discussion items and decision-making chores early on, and leave announcements and reminders for the end of the meeting. People really need the social aspect of meetings to maximize their creativity and their cooperation.

Third, follow an agenda distributed several days before, but allow members to modify it near the start of the meeting. The agenda will consist of items related to the **meeting start up** (introduction of new members or guests, appropriate humor, brief inspirational thoughts related to the cause, and review of the agenda). This will be followed by the **main content** of the meeting (discussion items, problem solving, goal setting, progress reports, follow-up, etc.). Finally, include **one-way communication** items (reports, announcements, reminders, etc.) followed by a **wrap-up** (review of assignments accepted, decisions made, decisions still pending, and information about the next meeting).

Fourth, every meeting should have a focus on progress toward goals. Goal setting, which we will discuss in the chapter that follows, will be a powerful motivating force. These goals will have an opposite effect, however, if the team does not produce an action plan and monitor their progress toward their goals. Sometimes, there may be a reason to celebrate team accomplishments. In other cases, it will involve problem solving if goals are not being accomplished. In all cases, the team must use meetings to discuss progress toward their goals.

A **final** element of positive meetings is the follow-up. All participants should receive minutes shortly after each meeting. The minutes will remind participants of what was accomplished in the meeting, as well as reminding them of things they need to do before the next one. Early on, ask participants if the minutes need to be more detailed, or less so. Together, you can get minutes that are very useful and that keep people on target in the meetings.

Conclusion

Meetings and other forms of interaction are an important part of developing effective teams. They will be only as effective as you make them, however, as you build trust and empower your team members. If their participation is expected and valued, and if they have significant input into the content, the meeting will be as much theirs as it is yours. You will see them begin to hold themselves responsible for results and develop a deep concern for what were once your problems. In the end, however, the children and the community will be the major benefactors. They must also be helped to own results. Applying the principles and skills presented can help you truly become a leader rather than just a manager.

Application Exercises

The following exercises are designed to help you apply the principles and skills presented in this chapter. But, they are more than just exercises. Like the exercise on determining our cause (Chapter One), they are essential elements in building a strong team and helping child care professionals develop ownership of their work and their relationships among themselves and with the community. Exercises like this are first steps in building a team.

A. Personal Reflection Exercise:

1. Mechanic or Gardener?[12]

Carefully ponder the following questions about your work as a leader:

1. How much do you trust each of the people with whom you work most directly? Are you best at finding their strengths or their weaknesses?

2. What decisions are you making without them that will require their knowledge, their cooperation, or their commitment? How much say do they really have in these decisions?

3. What evidence is there that people are afraid to take risks with you in suggesting solutions, or in trying to find their own solutions? How do you usually respond to "honest mistakes" (good efforts that have bad results)? Do your people really feel free to challenge your opinions and proposed solutions?

4. Are you primarily a "gardener" in your leadership role, or do you most often act as a "mechanic?" Are you more interested in helping people grow, or in making your organization run smoothly?

5. Do the members of your team feel frequent and heartfelt affirmation and appreciation from you?

Reflection Exercise 2.

Who Should Have Made This Decision?

As you examine the following account, determine whether the director in this program should have involved her staff in the decision she made. What do you think the result would have been had she chosen to do so?

> Our Center Director wanted us to "look professional" so she put a dress code in place. There are many problems with her dress code. First of all, we cannot afford to dress as nice as she wants us to. Then, we do not want to ruin our good clothes. The babies spit up all the time, and the toddlers' hands are not always clean when they touch us. I don't want to tell the children not to touch me. I am not comfortable on the floor in a skirt, and my shoes get rocks in them from the playground. I think that it puts me in a bad mood. I just don't feel comfortable, and it effects how I do my job. I want to hold the babies and play on the floor and sit in the sandbox, but not in the clothes I have to wear because of the dress code. I think I would do a better job if I felt comfortable.

B. Group Exercises
1. Defining failure. Try this activity with your child care professional's:
1. Ask everyone to write their definition of failure. This can be as broad as the failure of your agency, or failure in a particular area.
2. Each person should turn to the person at her side, sharing the definition that each wrote.
3. These two people combine their definitions to make one.
4. Those two then join with another pair to combine the definition of each group.
5. Continue this process until the entire group has ONE definition of failure.
6. This needs to be the definition of failure that the organization accepts.

2. Establishing Ground Rules

Overview: Ground rules are standards that a group determines regarding how they will treat each other. If a group chooses, they can also deal with how the group will interact with parents and people from the community. It is perhaps best to begin with the first category, standards regarding how you will treat each other. Next add ground rules related to your relations with the parents in your community at a later time.

Preparation: Give team members plenty of time to think about this. You may wish to have a preparation meeting in which you describe what you will be doing and explain why it is important. Do **not** let that meeting start to generate ground rules. Tell them that each individual needs time to prepare. Everyone should come to the next meeting prepared to contribute at least two ground rules. Get the group to choose one of the team to be the facilitator for this activity.

Activity: The facilitator may wish to have people work together in groups (4 - 6 people per group), or it may be best to have everyone work as a whole. This will depend upon the size of the entire group. Remember, it is important that everyone participate. The facilitator will apply the principles and skills outlined in this chapter to get the entire group to come to a consensus about what ground rules will be adopted. Try to keep the number of ground rules to a number between 5 and 10. Make sure you have achieved consensus before stopping, even if it means finishing it in another meeting. Consensus is reached when everyone agrees they can both live with and support the ground rules.

3. Problem Solving

Have your team meet to discuss a problem they would like to work on, both as an exercise and as a real problem that needs their attention. Make sure it is one that can be done "in house," or whose solution they can carry out without having to get permission from higher-ups. If you have difficulty coming up with a problem that fits this description, we suggest that you consider the following areas in which problems frequently occur in early childhood centers:

    * Parent Issues. (For example, are our expectations unrealistic?)

    * Children's Issues. (For example, what behavioral problems are most common?)

    * Child care professional Issues. (For example, how do we deal with unrealizable
        behavior?)

    * Organizational Issues. (For example, is this the best way to
        divide up the work?)

Follow the process outlined in the Problem Solving portion of the chapter to solve whichever problem your team identifies.

Chapter Notes

1. Stephen R. Covey, *Principle-Centered Leadership* (New York: Simon and Schuster, 1990).

2. Covey, *Principle-Centered Leadership*, 59.

3. Robert Rosenthal and Lenore Jacobson, *Pygmalion in the Classroom* (New York: Holt, Rinehart, and Winston. 1968

4. Kurt Lewin "Group decision and social change" in T, Newcomb and E. hartley (Eds.), *Readings in Social Psychology* (New York: Holt, Rinehart and Winston), 1950.

5. David Langford, Starlink Teleconference, "Quality and Education: Critical Linkages," October 12, 1993.

6. Our discussion of Structured Creativity is based largely on Dennis Romig, *Breakthrough Teamwork: Outstanding Results Using Structured Teamwork* (Chicago: Irwin Professional Publishing, 1996), 81.

7. Adapted from Belasco and Stayer, 60-63.

8 Romig, *Breakthrough Teamwork*.

9. The box is based on Jerry B. Harvey, *The Abilene Paradox* (Lexington Books, 1988).

10. We want to thank Kathy de la Peña, one of our graduate students, for this quote.

11. Romig, *Breakthrough Teamwork*.

12. We are indebted to Duncan and Pinegar, *Leadership for Saints*, for this distinction.

Chapter Five.
"Getting Where We Need to Go."
Principles of Strategic Planning

Chapter Summary

This chapter guides readers through principles and processes needed to move a team from building a sense of cause (and their particular mission in that cause) to clarifying a vision of where they wish to go, identifying clear objectives that will take them there, creating a plan for how to achieve these objectives, and setting up a system for monitoring results and making necessary adjustments.

Introduction

Teacher Martha Rodriguez crouches near the 2-year-old sand diggers at Manhattan's Bank Street Family Center, gently negotiating the rights to a suddenly special yellow rake. As Rodriguez bargains, the toddlers spin new connections to the brain area that controls "gimme now" impulses, connections that could very well later be used to ratchet up their SAT scores or their job-interviewing skills. Head teacher Lisa Farrell explains that the doll in Cammy's hot grip is really Caroline's from home, hence her classmate's avalanche of tears. Cammy's brain is wiring up to read other people's feelings, a skill she'll need to navigate through future relationships. A third teacher leads the diaper-dependent kids, one by one, to the changing table, exchanging coo for coo, babble for babble. Each child's neural circuits are carving highways in the brain where future vocabulary words will later travel with ease....Brain research underscores what educators have long argued: early social and emotional experiences are the seeds of human intelligence.[1]

It's wonderful to work in the field of early childhood development. Every day, science is revealing the enormous influence that early childhood experiences can have on young minds. Our's truly is a great cause. Early childhood educators are enormously influential on the intellectual, moral, physical, and social development of children. In addition, they empower parents, many of whom are marginalized from other social accomplishments, to succeed in what will eventually matter most in their lives—their parental responsibility.

This is our cause. It's what gets us up in the morning and what enables us to put up with frustration, dirty diapers, an environment of poverty, and parents who are struggling to find their way out of failure. But unless we are deeply and regularly connected to a sense of this cause, we risk burnout.

Researchers have found that a deep sense of commitment to something really important can carry you through even the hardest of times. One of America's foremost biographers, Studs Terkel, found this to be the case when he interviewed hundreds of people from many walks of life. His interviews revealed that the individuals most able to resist burnout are those who feel a deep sense of cause.

In his book *Working*[2], Terkel reported that persons employed in the helping professions (schools, medicine, etc.) have to endure serious frustration and stress. Those able to cope believe that their work has a higher purpose than just putting food on the table. They feel they are part of a very important cause and this keeps them going even when their work is frustrating and tough. A sense of cause is an anchor to the soul midst the frustrations of uncooperative children, bureaucratic regulations, and plugged-up toilets. It enables one to hold on in even the most trying circumstances.

Victor Frankl also discovered this. Mr. Frankl was a prisoner in a concentration camp during World War II. He survived near-starvation, disease, freezing cold, and brutality by hanging on to the belief that the psychiatry book he was writing would help mankind. Humans, he concluded, can survive virtually any circumstance if they have a sense of purpose, or commitment to a cause larger than themselves.

Developing a strong sense of cause is vital to the process of building team management in your organization. This process, often called **strategic planning**, can generate strong commitment from, and inspire the creativity of, everyone in your organization. Unfortunately, really *effective* strategic planning is rare. Often, it is an exercise in frustration. People are called together, told to come up with a strategic plan, given a cookie-cutter formula to follow, expected to say how they'll implement someone else's goals, and then find that nothing changes when they submit their plan. Obviously, this sort of planning is counter-productive.

Productive strategic planning has two main characteristics. First, it originates with a team that is empowered to chart its course. Second, it emphasizes "linkages." This means that all members of the team must clearly see the linkage between where they are going and what they must do to get there. One of your primary roles as a leader is to help them understand these linkages. Do they understand, for example, the linkage between a positive interaction with parents and the creation of strong families? Do they realize that there is a linkage between getting correct information on children and their healthy development? Do they see the linkage between carefully planned and executed activities and the improved quality of life for children and families?

Figure 5.1

You must help each other as a team to clearly see and always remember these linkages. A brief overview of the following figure will point out some of the main elements of strategic planning and the linkages that everyone must come to understand.

Starting from the bottom of figure 5.1, for example, everyone must have a firm sense of a shared cause. They must then see the linkage between this cause and the more specific mission of your agency. The difference between a cause and a mission is purely a matter of degree. Generally, a cause is seen as the larger good we serve, while a mission is the specific focus of our agency. In this context, helping children develop their enormous potential would be one way of stating our cause. The mission statement would describe the specific purposes, or place of our agency in this cause.

An image of a platoon in combat might clarify this difference. Their cause could be the freedom and well-being of their people. The mission, however, is their particular place in that cause, which might be to hold a particular position, to win a specific battle, or to carry a message to another unit.

While this distinction is a matter of focus, it is often important. What is the mission of your organization in the struggle to ensure the healthy development and well-being of children? Is there a particular community you serve? Do you only work with children, or do you help adults become better parents? Questions like these point toward a more focused mission.

From this sense of cause and the corresponding idea of your mission, you should develop a vision of what you want to achieve. A vision looks to the future, depicting specific accomplishments that you see taking place over a specific time period. What will you accomplish in five years, for example? What will your relations be like with each other and with the community you serve? What level of quality will you achieve?

As Figure 5.1 shows, once your team has determined this general vision, you must then link it to specific accomplishments that will be needed to make it happen. This process involves setting objectives which should be clear and specific statements of outcome. Your objectives are the essential accomplishments needed to bring about your vision.

Having developed clear objectives, you can then proceed to the most important stage of strategic planning-that of formulating a clear plan. Your plan is the linkage that spells out how you will accomplish your objectives. It lays down your method and describes what actions, programs, or procedures must be taken to accomplish these objectives.

As everyone knows, plans invariably conflict with reality to some extent. Though planning is essential to success, people and things can still be somewhat unpredictable. A person you count on will find another job. A grant may fail to come through. A machine may break down. Schools in your neighborhood might close. Laws may change. Existing funding sources may dry up. As a team, you need to adapt to these possibilities by closely monitoring your progress and solving problems even before they arise.

This process, summarized in Figure 5.1, need not be overly complicated. If you have completed the exercise on determining your cause (from the preceding chapter), you are well underway. In the sections that follow, we will guide you through the remaining points of this process. As you work on strategic planning as a team, you will create a positive culture and a sense of group loyalty that will build motivation. It really is essential for creating a team approach to managing early childhood centers.

Your Mission-Refining What You Stand For

In the 1960s, an interesting research project set up a measurement scale by which events that produce great stress in our lives could be measured and compared. They assigned a point value to many of the stressful changes and experiences that an individual might go through. The really traumatic events, like the death of a spouse, for example, received 100 points. Positive events, such as getting married, taking a vacation, or getting a promotion, were also assigned points, though at a lower level.

The researchers found that individuals who scored 300 points in a single year ran a very high risk of emotional or physical breakdown. Indeed, even individuals with scores between 150 and 300 ran a 50 percent chance of serious physical or emotional illness.

Years later, two other researchers set out to explain an apparent contradiction in the data. Some executives had scored above 300 points year after year, yet they never experienced a breakdown. In spite of constant relocations, promotions, and major life changes, they, like the Energizer Bunny(r), just kept going.

So the researchers set out to find out why. Using in-depth interviews and a battery of tests, they found that all of the "hardy" executives had a strong commitment to a personal mission in their lives. This sense of mission helped them view changes as challenges, rather than something threatening. As a result, these executives felt more in control of what was happening-not just helpless victims.[3]

This same approach to life works doubly well for teams. Team members can help each other keep their mission clearly in sight, thus more easily resisting stress. In addition, as their leaders empower them to accomplish the mission, they, like the executives just mentioned, will also feel more in control of the work that they do.

Why Create a Mission Statement? Empowerment centered on a mission creates a powerful force. People believe what they are doing really matters and that they are trusted to produce results that will take them there. This is why a mission statement should not be decided "on high" and handed down. It must be carefully worked out by those who will be doing the work. They must have substantial input into the decisions that affect where they are going and how they will get there. A good mission statement, worked out by a team, produces strong internal motivation and allows individuals to avoid burnout through a sense of control over where the group is going.

This is not to say, however, that every employee in an organization has to be involved in formulating a single mission statement. In larger organizations, top management may work as a team to formulate a mission statement for the organization. This mission statement is then used at lower levels by workers and leaders who set about formulating a mission statement for their own division. Still, the more interconnected all levels are in the formulation of mission statements, the better. Remember, we are trying to break down barriers among different divisions-not create new ones by working in isolation or at cross purposes.

The creation of a mission statement is one of the most important exercises your team will undertake. It is something that empowers team members, creates a sense of team spirit, and provides strong intrinsic motivation through a sense of ownership and empowerment. The work you have already done on defining your cause will help a great deal in developing the mission statement. The two are closely connected, and the mission flows out of a larger sense of cause. Like the statement of cause, the elaboration of your mission statement will be a useful application of the procedures of structured brainstorming previously presented.

Elements of a Powerful Mission Statement. Above all, a good mission statement must create excitement. It should be inspiring, compelling, and even passionate. Then, it will exist not just on paper, but will become deeply embedded in the hearts and minds of team members. It should energize them and tell anyone else what you stand for. It captures idealism and creates a sense of excitement about your work.

Let's look at a few examples. The Disney Corporation identified their mission for Disneyland as "creating the most wonderful place in the world." In the 1950s, the Sony Corporation decided they would "become the company most known for changing the worldwide poor-quality image of Japanese products." One school district proclaimed, "We empower children to become caring, competent, and responsible citizens who love to learn." Wal-Mart decided that their mission was "to give ordinary folk the chance to buy the same things as rich people," and Mary Kay Cosmetics proclaimed a mission "to give unlimited opportunity to women." One community agency that sponsored several early childhood programs for low-income families described their mission as follows: "Our mission is to improve the quality of life, and the self-sufficiency of families in our community."

Though not all mission statements are one-liners like these, the best ones always concisely convey what they stand for in a way that creates excitement. The exercise at the end of this chapter will further guide you in creating a good mission statement.

Do not worry if the statement of your cause is very similar to your mission statement. In fact, you want the two to be closely connected. The idealistic purpose you identified as the cause should carry over to your mission statement. Indeed, you may not need to maintain the statement of cause if you have truly incorporated its idealism into your mission statement. Do not abandon this sense of cause entirely, however. Remember that all meetings should have a brief portion (usually at the beginning) in which you remind each other of the cause. If your mission statement does this, then it rather than the cause statement, can be the focus of these presentations.

Your Vision—Seeing Where You're Going and What You'll Be Like

Once you have a clear idea of what you stand for, your team should develop a vision that looks to a specific future point in time. A vision statement helps you visualize together where and how you will be in a specified number of years. A **vision** is *a positive and idealistic description of the future that incorporates the deepest values and beliefs related to your cause and your mission.* Your vision describes how your organization will grow in the future and what your relationships will be like as a team and with the people you serve. A clear vision helps you translate your purpose into a sense of the direction that all members of the team can accept and to which they can become committed.

Before describing how to produce this vision, let's briefly consider a debate among strategic planners about whether the vision statement should be developed before or after a mission statement. Though this debate has some elements of the "Which came first—chicken or egg?" argument, we feel strongly that you should determine your cause and your mission before formulating your vision statement. Your vision about where you are going must be based on a clear idea of what you stand for. It should incorporate your most basic values. Otherwise, it will lead to aimless wandering or self-serving grand-standing. Let's examine the following parable to illustrate this point.

> The executive director of a large program took her supervisors to the top of a hill where they could see a valley spread out far below. She said to them, "Do you see that rise over there, beside the stream?"
>
> "Yes," they said, "we see it."
>
> She then asked them, "Can you picture a beautiful house on that rise? Can you visualize it?"
>
> "Yes, we can imagine it," they replied.
>
> "Now picture acres and acres of manicured lawns and a swimming pool in the back. Can you see that also?"
>
> "Yes," they exclaimed, "we see that also."
>
> Then, she turned to them and said, "If you work really hard for the next few years and help me double my salary, some day all that will be mine."[4]

A vision that really motivates and empowers workers must be based on the pursuit of *shared* values. These will be identified during the team meetings in which you define your cause and your mission. If you have a clear idea about the cause in which all of you are collectively involved, as well as your part in advancing that cause, you can move toward a future that incorporates these values and deeply-held beliefs. Thus, any move toward the future must be guided by powerful feelings concerning what you stand for as a team or as an organization. This vision becomes the way you will accomplish a greater *common* good.

Though this look into the future is, of course, somewhat idealistic, it must also be grounded in reality. It should not be just a dream about what you *could* accomplish—but a down-to-earth examination of what you *can and will* bring to pass. In essence, you are planning backwards. You mentally picture yourselves at some future date admiring what you have become. You ask yourself from this future perspective how you arrived from where you are today. This helps you envision the type of organization you propose to become, but it is not idle daydreaming. It asks what this future will be like as you struggle with the same problems, limitations, and personality issues that you currently face.

Your vision should describe this future from several points of view. Which major accomplishments will you attain as an organization? What level of quality will you achieve? What will be the character of the relationships you have with each other and with your client community? What degree of parental involvement will you attain? Which chronic problems will you have solved or reduced?

Your vision should include *some* reaching for the stars, "dreaming the impossible dream," as it were. At the same time, they should be grounded in reality. A great vision asks a lot of you, but it should be achievable, at least in a general way. One great leader said, "Vision without work is dreaming. Work without vision is drudgery. Work coupled with vision is destiny."[5]

Your objectives, or goals, represent bite-sized steps toward accomplishing your vision, so don't make your vision too specific. A vision is what you reach toward. Your objectives are what you will actually reach. In this way, your vision will always stretch out before you, inspiring effort and helping you to set and accomplish objectives that take you there. Vision is your projected journey, while your goals or objectives are the mileposts and the accomplishments along the way.

Setting Realistic Objectives

With a clear vision of where you want to go, and what you want to be, you can set objectives that will help take you there. Whereas vision is idealistic and something you will always strive for, objectives are practical and reasonable. You set objectives with a strong commitment to achieve them. Goals and objectives are much more task oriented. However, these tasks are the benchmarks that mark the way toward accomplishing your vision. Your goals and objectives clearly state the accomplishments that must be attained if you are to make your vision a reality.

We should point out that many advocates of strategic planning distinguish between goals and objectives. We do not. The difference they propose is in the level of generality, one set being more specific than the other. We believe a good vision statement will provide you with the general level. Objectives (call them goals if you want) will represent the more specific level.

Though goals should be focused on measurable accomplishments, there is a danger in representing these objectives as quotas or numerical "targets." This danger is illustrated by Texas schools, and those of other states, in which performance ratings are based on achievement test scores (the TAKS in Texas, for example). Teachers in many schools spend much time and effort "teaching the test," often to the exclusion of teaching the children. Because achievement test scores are used to determining rankings, administrators set "targets" for each school. A common result is that children are drilled for hours at a time on test questions with little real learning.

Examples like these abound in industry as well. Several years ago, the Soviet Union found that it had a severe shortage of large nails. Upon investigation, it was discovered that someone had set a "quota" for the number of nails that should be manufactured each month in order to increase production. The nail factories, finding it much easier to meet this quota by producing small nails, had stopped making large ones altogether.

A similar thing happened recently in New York City. One Transit Police commander set up a quota for the number of arrests his officers should make, thinking it was a good indicator of their performance. Their ratings, and eventually their promotions and choice of assignments, depended on how well they filled these quotas. Some time later, it was discovered that the "highest performing" officers had made many false and illegal arrests. Most of these arrests were of Black and Hispanic men, because they had less clout with which to defend themselves. When the situation came to light, most of the convictions by these officers, whether legitimate or illegitimate, had to be thrown out. The quotas had a far more destructive effect on the community and on the Transit Police than could be justified by any good they might have accomplished.

Early childhood programs often run into the same problem, as the following account illustrates:

> Head Start programs are required to examine a child's absences when they dip below an 85% attendance level. In one program, this requirement became an absolute standard for everyone enrolled in the program, including home-based families. So when a family canceled a home visit, or was not home when the visit was scheduled, the agency required the home visitor to reschedule the visit so that they would "meet the requirement." This caused multiple problems for the agency staff in scheduling. It also sent the message to the families that they could cancel anytime because they would just be rescheduled for another visit. As a result, it became a logistical nightmare for the home-visiting staff.

We are not saying that you should never set numerical goals. Just be sure that the effort to meet these goals does not accomplish them at the expense of your organization or of its mission and your vision for it. One way to avoid this is to make sure that people who will be expected to accomplish your goals, the team members, set them. Also, make sure these goals flow from the cause, the mission, and the vision previously set.

Another way to avoid the dangers of numerical goals becoming quotas is to set objectives that propose **direction** to where you want to go. For example, rather than saying that you will increase the number of volunteer parents by 30 percent, you might set a goal "to substantially increase the quantity and the quality of participation by parents." You could still set standards of how you will measure the attainment of these goals, but without locking yourselves into artificial numbers. In fact, if you truly have a commitment to the mission and to your vision for the organization, numerical goals will be less important than your sense, as a team, of how well you are accomplishing your most important values.

Do not avoid numerical objectives altogether, however. Just be sure that the measures of your progress really measure your objectives. If you say you want to increase parental involvement by 30 percent, how will you measure it? Will it be the number of parents that sign up as volunteers? Will you count the number of hours that parents actually help out? Anytime you set goals and objectives, you need to measure your progress. Just be careful that the measures don't become quotas. Otherwise, people will attempt to increase the measure, perhaps at the expense of the objective.

This may be what happened with the transit police. The number of arrests was a measure of how hard each officer was supposed to be working. Unfortunately, when the commander stopped paying attention to other indicators of hard work, the objective became a quota with very destructive effects.

Goals and objectives are most effective when everyone is aware of them and of the progress they are making. For this reason, it is best to keep the quantity of objectives to a manageable number. We recommend that you set no more than six goals initially (though in subsequent years you may be able to increase that to eight). These objectives should be stated concisely, with ways built in to measure your progress on a regular basis. A major portion of team meetings should be dedicated to analyzing how well you are accomplishing your objectives, and whether the measures really reflect your progress.

We also recommend that you determine which one or two of your objectives are the most important. Sometimes, reaching of particular objectives makes it much easier to accomplish others. It is a very useful team exercise to distinguish what the primary goals are. Once this has been determined, you should give them the most attention in your meetings.

In your meetings, you should also give a great deal of attention to discussing your progress towards your goals. These discussions should highlight your progress and will be highly motivating. On such occasions, you should celebrate your successes. Be very careful, however, not to celebrate phony successes. You are trying to build a culture of excellence. When a small or insignificant accomplishment is made to appear grand, you are telling your team that you are not really serious about excellence. It takes patience, but it lets everyone know that you are not interested in making the mediocre appear grandiose. Celebrating phony successes only lower their confidence in being able to do something truly remarkable.

If you are having problems achieving the goals, team meetings should be dedicated to problem solving. Make sure, however, that looking for ways to get back on track in these meetings does not turn into finger pointing. Problem solving is not about finding someone to blame. Train your team in the principles and techniques of problem solving (we discuss these in a later chapter). Then, let them take ownership for finding solutions.

Developing and Implementing a Plan of Action

Of all the work you do together as a team, nothing is more important than working together to come up with your **plan** for accomplishing your objectives. Your plan, of course, flows from your objectives, which in turn came from your vision, your mission and your cause. You have the responsibility to see that these are living documents, and not pieces of paper or signs hanging on the wall. Don't put your people through these exercises if you are not committed to using them as anchors against which all future decisions will be measured. One of the most de-motivating experiences you can give your team is to get them excited about accomplishing certain objectives, and then fail to determine the plan by which you will accomplish these goals together.

As you work out your plan, you will be answering the question, "By what method will we accomplish our objectives?" It is also wise to determine which individuals will have primary responsibility for keeping you on track with your plan, though you want to make sure that everyone feels ownership for devising a plan and then ensure it is working.

If your objectives were more specific than the previous stages of strategic planning, the plan is more specific still. In your plan, you will specifically identify what is needed to accomplish each objective, who will be primarily responsible, which actions will occur first, and what resources will be made available.

In reality, the plan spells out the tactics by which the goals will be achieved. While the plan is also a team effort, team members will be the primary players called upon to accomplish specific objectives and should have the greatest say in what tactics they will use to accomplish these objectives. At the very least, make sure that you have achieved true consensus about the plan from team members who will be asked to carry out particular objectives.

The action plan lays out the steps that must be taken to accomplish each objective. Often, these steps will be listed under each objective, although some steps will be used for more than one objective. The plan also identifies the strategies that will be used and a projected timeframe for accomplishing each step. It also identifies what resources will be required for accomplishing these steps and how these resources will be secured. In sum, the action plan is a very specific outline of what will be done to accomplish your objectives (see the exercise at the end of the chapter for more details).

Measurement and Problem Solving

As you begin to implement your plan, you will need to have in place key indicators that will show how well you are accomplishing your objectives. These indicators not only measure your progress (or lack of it), but help you identify problems when they are still manageable. Many well-planned organizations have faltered because they failed to identify ways of gauging their progress or identifying problems in the early stages.

When you have these measures clearly visible to all team members, everyone can help spot problems before they become serious issues. This helps create ownership. Anyone who spots a problem should be expected to begin taking steps to solve it. This overcomes a classic weakness of many organizations—the idea that the manager or the supervisor is the person responsible for solving problems. The team must be encouraged to own problems, just as they must have ownership for the objectives and the plan. Otherwise, as we pointed out with the opening case in Chapter Four, they will bring you all the problems and wash their hands of the responsibility for finding solutions.

We'll say more about problem solving in Chapter Six. Our main emphasis here is the need to identify or create effective measures of progress in accomplishing your objectives. This process should also be a team process. They will be familiar with the measures already available and are in a good position to judge whether a particular indicator really measures how well you are accomplishing an objective.

Let us look at an example. The First Progress Report on Head Start Program Performance Measures[6] lists several objectives for Head Start. The first objective listed was to have the children in Head Start demonstrate clear improvement in emergent literacy, numeracy, and language skills. What measures are available to show how well Head Start programs are accomplishing this objective? What existing data sources are available? To measure how well a particular program is accomplishing this objective, we should identify what assessment measures are already in place or the sources of data or information available. They identify, for example, child assessment instruments, ongoing parent interviews, or teacher ratings as measures of each child's progress.

Another objective identified was that Head Start children will receive medical, dental, and mental health services. The measures they propose as indicators of progress are data obtained from the PIR and the MSMTS, which will be used to show the number and percentage of children who receive medical services, dental services, immunizations, and mental health services.

Whatever sources of data you chose must be consistent and ongoing. In other words, you need a measure that shows each child's performance as he or she begins the program and at regular intervals thereafter. These measures need to be consistent, measuring the same type of information at each point in time. Otherwise, you will be attempting to compare apples with oranges.

Many of the measures you use will already be available from the data you have been collecting all along. When you have no data source, the team may need to develop a new measure. As you do so, however, try to eliminate data sources that are not being used so that you do not overwhelm your team with too much data and too many measures. Often, such a review can eliminate some measures that serve no useful purpose.

As you examine your needs for measuring progress, keep in mind that most indicators or data sources only measure part of what you need to know. As a result, you will often need to have more than one indicator, or measure of each objective. Try to use subjective measures (opinions and verbal statements, for example) as well as objective measures (numbers, percents, etc.). Together, these indicators will give a more complete picture of the progress you are making. This will also help you avoid turning numerical indicators into quotas.

This last point is very important. Indicators are important, but we shouldn't mistake them for the real thing. Parental involvement, for example, is an important objective. If you use an indicator like the number of hours parents spend in your center as the only indicator of it, however, you will miss many other forms of parental involvement. Keep asking your team if the measures you are using truly reflect the progress you are making toward your objectives, your vision, your mission, and your shared cause. This periodic "reality check" keeps you from becoming so involved in numbers that you forget what you are really all about.

Chapter Application Exercises
A. Personal Reflection Exercises[7]
Exercise 1: Clarifying Your Roles

Take a piece of paper and write down as many of your personal roles as you can. If you're an adult female, for example, this might include something like, mother, wife, friend, neighbor, daughter, sister, program director, PTA president, etc. If you think about it long enough, you can probably come with a list of 20 or more roles. Now take three or four of your most important roles and break each down into its sub-roles. Your role as mother, for example, might include coach, teacher, friend, referee, chauffeur, accountant, nurturer and so forth. Now, reflect on what you have listed. As you have listed these roles and sub-roles, you have actually been addressing your values. Listing nurturer, for example, means you value this part of your role as a mother. It should also say something about how you would really like to use your time. Next, take the sub-roles that are most important to you and list the character traits that you feel are needed to support this sub-role. All of this will help you clarify, or even rediscover, your values. Finally, ask yourself if you are spending adequate time and resources on the things that you value most.

Exercise 2: Your Personal Mission-Vision Statement

This exercise builds on the one just completed and is designed to help you bring your life into better focus and balance. It will allow you to clarify who you are and what is genuinely important to you. It will also serve as a screening device that allows you to determine which activities deserve more attention and which to eliminate or reduce that you are simply responding to without much thought or reflection.

Start with a clean sheet of paper. On top of it, write "First Draft." Next, write down what causes are most important to you (you might refer to your list of roles and sub-roles for ideas). Now, write several versions of what you consider your most important mission(s) in life. Focus here on what you feel is most important for you to do in life. Next, write a statement that reflects what you want to be, or become. You may now put these into a single statement, or you may want to have three-one of your cause, another of your mission, and a third of your vision for your future.

Refer to this document frequently, especially when you feel yourself getting caught up in the routine of daily activities. This will allow you to take greater control of your life. You begin to manage it-not just drift along letting less important things control you. It is based on the philosophy that too many good activities are the greatest obstacle to achieving those which are truly essential.

B. Team Exercises

Exercise 1. Developing a Powerful Mission Statement

Preparation: 1) Have the team members read the section in this chapter entitled, "Your Mission-Refining What You Stand For" prior to the session. 2) Ask them to each come prepared with a one- or two-sentence statement that answers the questions: *What is the specific focus, or mission, of our agency as it relates to the cause we are engaged in as early childhood workers?* Their statements should start with the words, *"Our mission is to* _____. 3) Appoint one of the group members as the facilitator and make sure she is thoroughly familiar with the role of a facilitator described in this chapter.

Activity: 1) Have the facilitator briefly assemble everyone. Together, the group should discuss the power of a great cause, described in Chapter Two. Someone, perhaps one of your best teachers, should present a discussion about the motivating power of a great cause. **2)** The entire group will then be subdivided into groups, with 4 - 6 individuals per group. Each group will select a "scribe" to write down their final statement-one or two sentences that summarize the cause to which early childhood workers should be committed. The statement should be powerful and inspire a sense of great importance in the work done. **3)** Next, bring everyone back together and get the scribe for each group to read their statements. **4)** Finally, use the skills outlined in this chapter (structured creativity and developing consensus) to come up with a team consensus of your cause. Do all you can to make it something that communicates a sense of great importance, with wording that inspires commitment to the cause. Keep it short but powerful.

Chapter Notes

1 LynNell Hancock and Pat Wingert, "The New Preschool," *Newsweek*, Spring/Summer 1997, 36.

2 Studs Terkel, *Working: People Talk About What They Do All Day And How They Feel About It* (New York: The New Press, 1972).

3 Dennis Romig, *Breakthrough Teamwork* 1996, citing the research of T.H. Holmes and R.H. Rahe (1967) and that of S.R. Maddi and S.C. Kobasa (1984).

4 Based on a similar fictitious account in Belasco and Stayer, 1993, 94, 95.

5 Thomas S. Monson, as quoted in Duncan and Pinegar, *Leadership for Saints*, 65.

6 Source:http://www2.acf.dhhs.gov/programs/hsb/research/progrpt1/framwork.htm.

7 These exercise are adapted from Duncan and Pinegar, *Leadership for Saints*, 52 - 55.

Chapter Six.
Building Effective Relationships

Chapter Summary

Good relationships are built upon many of the principles discussed in other chapters. This chapter shows how these principles, and some related skills, can be used to create effective relationships. These include empowerment, ownership, staying focused on your mission, seeking win-win solutions, and having high expectations. The skills and practices include interviewing skills, effective communications, negotiation and conflict resolution, and administering effective discipline.

Introduction

You knew when you were called from his office, it was not good. He intended to show you he was in charge. There was a horrible lack of communication. He and two cronies were like the three top dogs who made the decisions. And, they might never tell you what they decided. Their attitude was, "You won't know until we tell you, and you'll only know what we think you need to know."

This guy was a champion for children. He would get down on the floor with them, but he just did not connect with the folks he worked with. His meetings were very predictable. Everyone would give one "positive" from their work. Then, you'd go though his agenda. If you were ever late to a meeting or missed part of it, he would remind you in a very public kind of way. If you overspent or you do not monitor your budget, you'd hear about it (and so would everyone else). But if you improved and tried really hard to do better, the negative evaluation stayed on your record year after year.

We would wait to meet with him outside his office, and we would tease each other as we were waiting and say things like,

"What are you in for? Have you got any priors?" It felt like seeing the warden.

When he introduced you to someone outside the building, he would talk about you in such glowing terms that you wondered if he was introducing you! But, everyone knew. It was only a form of manipulation.

This otherwise capable man was inept in relationships. A landmark study[1] of why executives fail shows that this example is not an isolated case. The results indicate that the most frequently mentioned cause of executive failure is the inability to maintain good relationships. Those who are harshly critical, insensitive, or demanding alienate everyone with whom they work.

In another study, managers who were unsuccessful lacked empathy and sensitivity. Some could be charming on occasion, but they often used their charm to manipulate others. Many were highly insensitive. Instead of building a strong network of mutually beneficial relationships, they generated resentment and undermined the cooperation that was so vital to success.[2]

A study of what characteristics corporations look for in new MBAs demonstrates the same pattern. The three most desired capabilities for new managers are communication skills, interpersonal skills, and initiative.[3] Increasingly, employers are discovering that being able to maintain good relationships matters most for success on the job.

With this realization comes the question, "Can people who are weak in relationships improve substantially through training or coaching?" Research in the field of "emotional intelligence" strongly suggests that they can. Emotional intelligence has been defined as **"the capacity for recognizing our own feelings and those of others, for motivating ourselves, and for managing emotions well in ourselves and in our relationships."**[4] Unlike IQ, which tends to change very little after our teen years, emotional intelligence seems in large measure to be learned. Our competence in it can keep growing.[5]

Many people who are "book smart" end up working for people who, though having a lower IQ, are better at relationships. This is illustrated by the following account by the director of a consulting firm.

> I had the lowest cumulative grade point average in my engineering school. But when I joined the Army and went to officer candidate school, I was number one in my class-it was all about how to handle yourself, get along with people, work in teams, leadership. And that's what I find to be true in the world of work.[6]

How much does IQ predict success on the job? The most optimistic estimates propose that IQ only explains 25 percent of job success. Most studies don't even give it that much credit. The most pessimistic results claim that it only predicts 4 percent of those who succeed. Indeed, in some cases, it has a negative correlation. In one study of Harvard graduates in the fields of teaching, medicine, business, and law, scores on the entrance exam (a substitute measure of IQ) had zero or even a negative correlation with eventual career success.[7]

The ability to be effective in relationships is much more important than IQ. A great deal of research has established that the most effective leaders are effective, not so much because of expertise in their field, but due to the quality of relationships they are able to maintain.

Principles of Effective Relationships

Most of the principles of team management presented in the preceding chapters can be applied to building and maintaining strong relationships. Team management is not limited to meetings or to other group settings. Indeed, the most impressive accomplishments as a leader will not be made in front of the entire team, but in establishing your one-on-one relationships with individuals.

Being effective at relationships requires some important skills. Even more important than development of *skills*, however, is the ability to base relationships on sound principles. Let's briefly review how some of the key principles of team management presented earlier are correlated with sound interpersonal relationships. [8]

A *principle* is something that tells us where we want to go. It is a broad guideline that helps us determine what is appropriate and what is not. Programs and practices, in contrast, give us specific techniques and other means of getting there. It is a principle, for example, that parents should be involved to the greatest degree possible in early childhood programs. We come up with programs and practices in accordance with this principle to ensure success. However, we always keep the principle ahead of the specific programs and practices.

The Principles of Empowerment and Ownership. As you work with individuals, you should constantly work to empower them and get them to take ownership for their work and help them find solutions to the problems they experience. This, in itself, requires a change in the relationship between many managers and those who work "under them." A manager who feels the need to push people for results, or who wants to be in control, will have a difficult time doing this. So will managers who see themselves as the problem solvers of their organizations. Those who try to maintain control or to micro-manage solutions fail to empower their employees. As a result, their staff feels little ownership for their jobs and will perform far below their level of capability.

Empowerment and transferring ownership often require fundamental changes in relationships. These changes start by seeing yourself more as a colleague to the people who officially report to you, as opposed to thinking of yourself as their boss or supervisor. Indeed, you may want to limit your use of the term "supervisor," which suggests watching someone from a superior position. Instead, you become more of a coach and a mentor. In keeping with the sports analogy, it's probably better to think in terms of soccer than football. You don't want to be constantly "sending in plays" and micromanaging, even if it is from the sidelines. You insist that they make many of their own decisions in order for them to feel ownership. You must encourage people to develop ownership for their own work (and the problems they experience).

But it has to go even further than that. In order to use influence, as opposed to control, team members must sense that they have an influence on you. This requires a great deal of self-discipline on your part. You may need to train yourself to truly listen, to find value in what they say or do, and to be willing to let people make occasional mistakes as they grow. Though this is not easy to do, the dividends are enormous, both for your organization and the people you increasingly come to care about.

For many, this requires a major change in how they relate to others. We have to really care as much (sometimes even more) about their individual development as we do about getting results. The personal touch is extremely important in this area. It really is true that "people don't care how much you know until they know how much you care."

The Principle of Staying Focused on a Cause, a Mission, and a Shared Vision. Although it is vitally important for statements of cause, mission, and vision to be developed in a team setting, they will be effective only to the degree that they also form a central focus of your interaction as individuals. If not, you risk giving the impression that your vision and mission statements are only slogans. People expect us to be upbeat and take a high moral road in public settings. Then, they wait to see our more private behavior to determine whether we really mean what we say. This means we "walk the talk." The sentiments and vision worked out in public settings have to carry over to our one-on-one interaction.

The "reach-for-the-stars" aspect of the cause, the mission, and the vision are intertwined with relationships in another important way. A fundamental part of your organization's mission should be the well-being of the people with whom you work. Their well-being is either undermined or assured by the nature of your one-on-one relationships with them. You must reject manipulation and the use of force as ways to get people to do what needs doing. Rely instead on respect, allegiance to a common cause, and on other forms of intrinsic motivation. By the same token, if you want others to abide by the ground rules, they will have to gather from your daily interactions with them, that you hold yourself accountable to these rules as well.

While the *setting* may be different from team meetings, the principles are virtually the same. Drive out fear in relationships. People motivated by fear forget the cause and seek short-term *appearances*. Rather than looking for the best solutions, they try to please you, even if they know that what they *think* you want is wrong. In addition, if fear is a major motivator, they will work harder on finding ways to excuse themselves rather than on accomplishing what really needs to be done. They will also cease to search for solutions, preferring instead to bring everything to you. In sum, basing relationships on power and control makes some people aim to please you, or do just enough to stay out of trouble, rather than using their talents and knowledge to build children and families.

The Principle of Seeking Win-Win Solutions. Once you are on the high moral ground of putting a cause above your personal interests, you can generate enormous trust through win-win interactions. To illustrate, consider how you approach an interaction with a trusted doctor. You can place a great deal of trust in the doctor if you believe that she holds your well being as a very high priority. You will generally trust her judgment because you believe she is more interested in preserving your health than in getting your money. If you don't believe that, then you'll treat her much as you would door-to-door salesmen. With them, everything they say is suspect because you do not believe they have your best interest at heart.

Sound relationships must be built upon trust in order to produce benefits for everyone, especially the children you serve. This trust, like that you place in your physician, grows as each person comes to believe that others are motivated by a higher cause and by a commitment to win-win relationships. These relationships are those in which all parties are committed to maximizing the benefits of each other.

Stephen Covey[9] says that people who have a "scarcity mentality" take a "win-lose" approach to relationships. If there is only so much to go around ("zero sum," in the scarcity mentality), then what you get represents something that I must lose. If that is how someone thinks, they can never be happy for your success because it means your win is their loss.

Organizations with win-lose relationships and a "scarcity mentality" are not pleasant places to work. No one wants to share an idea for fear that someone else will get credit for it. People hoard resources, afraid that someone else will take them away. The well-being of clients (in our case, children) takes second place to protecting "turf." In addition, people engage in malicious gossip and find other ways to undermine whomever they see as a competitor.

If that is not the kind of life you want to live, then "win-win" has to be firmly built into all relationships. Cooperation replaces competition. We look out for each other and offer help without "keeping score." And above all, we are loyal to each other and to the cause we all serve. Both forms of loyalty are important to keep organizations from becoming corrupt "old-boy" networks where mutual back scratching is done at the expense of our cause and our clients.

The Pygmalion Principle, or the Principle of High Expectations. Another principle that flies in the face of boss-style management, one we introduced in Chapter Four, is learning to look hard for strengths in those we are assigned to "supervise." Bosses tend to see their roles as finding weaknesses and then getting people to correct them (though a "good" boss will be nice about it). Leaders, by contrast, find strengths in others and use the power of positive expectations to help people meet those expectations. Their relationships are very supportive because they base expectations on real strengths, rather than on insincere flattery or other manipulations.

To illustrate, consider an example proposed by Goleman.[10] He describes a situation faced by the U.S. Navy. Under-motivated, problem sailors were branded as "LPs," or low performers, by their supervisors. Instead of attempting to reform these sailors, the Navy set out to do something new—change the way their supervisors saw them. Despite serious reservations, the supervisors were taught to expect the best from problem sailors. They did not simply make up strengths or exaggerate minor ones. The supervisors instead found real strengths in the men. Then, on the basis of these strengths, supervisors communicated new expectations to the former "LPs," letting them know that they believed in their ability to change. As a result, the LP's began to perform better on every measure. They not only improved their overall performance, but many changed their personal appearance. This was the "Pygmalion Effect," or the tendency for high expectations to become a self-fulfilling prophecy.

The Pygmalion Effect is very powerful—so much so that it has spawned the Self- Esteem Movement. Unfortunately, this movement often fails to harness the power of positive expectations in producing positive behavior. Such failure happens when flattery and admonitions like, "You are special," are substituted for really raising expectations. These expectations must actually come up in the eye of you the beholder, or they will fail. Most people can see through manipulations. Worse, many come to believe that they also can manipulate approval with virtually no effort at all, or that they deserve special treatment because they are "so special."

For this reason, in all relationships leaders need to develop the ability to find real strengths. Part of this comes from seeing the worth of each person. If you see every child, for example, as a Divine creation with the potential for greatness, then you will not need to tell children they are "special" (especially if this infers that they are somehow better than non-special people).

You also need to believe that everyone, no matter how corrupted they may have become, has some good. If you don't really believe it's there, you won't search for it. Then, unless you actually find it, your expectations will fail to lift those who desperately need lifting.

An additional ability that needs to be developed to harness the Pygmalion Effect is being able to see obvious weaknesses in their proper perspective. Inspired leaders do not ignore dangerous weaknesses, nor do the pretend they do not exist. Rather, the leader keeps these in proper perspective. It's about seeing people as more than their stains. True leadership involves regarding the worker as a whole person and using that vision to help them to regard their flaws as something "out of character." Unless you actually see these strengths, however, you cannot help those you lead see themselves in a more positive light.

The surest way to harness the power of positive expectations is to develop an ability to find strengths in others, give them the coaching and encouragement needed, help them set and achieve high standards, then be there to share their victories. High expectations are about achieving excellence. You help people raise their sights, rather than lower standards by lavishing false praise on them.

Putting Principles ahead of Programs and Practices.

As we said earlier, principles provide broad guidelines regarding what is appropriate and what is not. As such, they guide our direction. Programs and practices, on the other hand, offer specific techniques for getting there. The relationship between principles and programs (or practices) can be seen in the way we undertake a journey. Knowing where you want to go must come before deciding the means you will use to get there. So, just as determining your mission and your vision must precede developing a plan (Chapter Five), focusing more on principles than programs & practices.

Sound principles allow us to be *effective*. Well-run programs and practices help us be *efficient*. During World War II, the Nazi military establishment proved itself to be highly efficient. In a very short time, it made shocking advances. However, these results were not based on sound principles. In terms of what matters most to human societies, it was not effective.

Similarly, some sales personnel may have skills that allow them to be very efficient in making sales. If they do so at the expense of the well-being of customers, however, they may be very ineffective at meeting the needs of those whose purchases support the seller. By the same token, early childhood programs that put good programs and practices above principles *may* become highly efficient. The danger is that they may make their gains in efficiency at the expense of effectiveness.

Unfortunately, many programs fail to be very good at either effectiveness or efficiency. Learning and internalizing sound principles will increase your effectiveness. Implementing sound skills and developing good programs based on principles will help you to become efficient as well.

There are other reasons to put principles ahead of programs. One of the most important is seen in the public schools. Every year in many districts, some new program or practice comes along that is often at odds with the one instituted just the year before. Teachers have to take valuable time away from their classes to attend workshops in which they must learn it. These new programs wear people out. They learn to give minimal attention to the newest fad, preferring instead to let it wear itself out. This constant changing of programs is enormously wasteful of time, resources, and morale. Unless there are some guiding principles, this change will confuse and exhaust your teachers. It will confuse and exhaust your teachers.

It is far better to base yourself on sound principles that govern how you will treat each other, the children in your care, and their parents. You may recognize that some of the ground rules you established are, in reality, nothing more than principles that lay out how you will treat each other. One of the most important ground rules, for example, might be that gossip and complaining to a third party will not be tolerated. Such a rule is based on the principle that people should try to resolve their conflicts before involving other people. As you implement the principle, you may collectively decide that the only time a third party should be involved is to help the process (but never to get allies).

Make a commitment to build all relationships in your organization on sound principles. This will help you avoid techniques that are manipulative or that produce short-term gains at the expense of long-term relationships. Before you implement any program, or even prior to giving your people training on some practice, make sure that you agree on the principles that these programs and practices will serve.

Finally, make sure that a great deal of the teaching and coaching that takes place in your organization is designed to teach sound principles. This will not happen in a single session, nor will it come mainly from a training seminar. It will happen as all of you "walk the talk," holding each other accountable to maintaining these principles. Don't expect others to follow ground rules or principles that you fail to follow. This, in reality, is the basis for transferring ownership and empowering workers at all levels. Once the people you lead truly internalize these principles (or hold themselves personally accountable to them), they will then be empowered to largely govern themselves.

Specific Skills Needed for Building Effective Relationships

Once leaders become effective in relationships by building them upon sound principles, they need the skills and techniques that will enable them to also be efficient in their work with people. Some skills can be quickly learned. Others will take considerable time and practice. Though the field of leadership development requires many skills, a few stand out as vital for managing early childhood programs. We will briefly outline these skills, recognizing that in order to become highly adept in them, most people will require considerable training, practice, and personal development.

One-on-One Interviewing. As a leader in early childhood programs, you are constantly interacting with people, occasionally in meetings, sometimes in small groups, and frequently alone with another individual. Though all such occasions are valuable, the time you spend one-on-one has the potential for achieving the greatest gains in your program. In part, this is because this setting, more than any other, allows you to respond directly to people and to learn the most about their capabilities and needs. It is also the setting where they will feel they can best come to know you. They will often base their views about you and your "true feelings" more on this setting than on your more public pronouncements.

The term "interview" may not always appropriately describe this interaction. Most of us think of an interview as a setting in which one person asks questions to get information from another. While this is certainly one use of an interview, such interaction does little for relationships. Our discussion here uses a much broader definition of "interview" to include all private one-on-one communications where two individuals interact, each in their organizational role. As Duncan and Pinegar[11] state, "The very best interviews don't really feel like 'interviews' at all. They feel like a comfortable visit with a trusted friend."

In this setting, you not only exchange information, but can potentially have a major impact on the people with whom you work (and they are allowed to have a similar impact on you). In this setting, you can motivate, discipline, inform, and empower your staff. It is also an excellent setting for problem solving, conflict resolution, personal goal setting, and accountability. When done well, it will be one of your most effective techniques for positively affecting your organization and its culture.

There are, of course, many types of interview formats. We will deal primarily here with the *non-directive* interview, a format that minimizes your authority over the person being interviewed, and that maximizes their ownership and empowerment. In team leadership, this form of interview is the most common. Your decision to occasionally use a more *directive* interview will be guided by the principles just discussed.

To be effective, you should approach each non-directive interview with certain assumptions. Perhaps foremost is the understanding that the interviewee, not you the interviewer, is responsible for herself. In essence, you assume that she is capable of solving her own problems, or setting her own goals, if given a little encouragement or coaching. Your primary role is to help her maintain ownership of her responsibility and empower her to use this authority wisely.

Though most people would not argue with this assumption, it is surprising how many interview situations quickly deteriorate into a situation where ownership for problems and responsibilities is shifted to the person in charge. Let's take a very common exchange to illustrate. One of your administrators comes into your office and says, *"I've had it with ____. She never comes to work on time and always has some lame excuse for not getting her work done. I don't see how I can continue working with her."* What is your initial response? If you're like most people, you'll probably start asking questions to become better informed about the situation. If you do, you risk taking responsibility away from the person who just described the problem. He/she is likely to think you are asking for information to make a decision. Even if you only want to offer suggestions, it implies that you are the problem solver and that people should bring their problems to you.

That doesn't mean you'll turn a deaf ear or rudely tell her to solve her own problems. Rather, you'll listen with empathy, acknowledge that the issue is important, and assure her of your confidence that she will deal effectively with the situation. Your job is not to solve the problem. It is to create an atmosphere where the interviewee can solve the problem. After listening with empathy, for example, you might ask something like, "What do you think you can do?" In many cases, you'll get an answer like, "I don't know. I've tried everything." This is a good time to remind her of other times when she managed to solve a difficult issue and assure her that you know she'll do it again.

Another important assumption that you must communicate in nondirective interviews is that people want to do the right thing when they see clearly what the right thing is *for them.* An effective solution must fit the person's own values, beliefs, goals, and needs, *as well as the values, goals and needs of the organization.* A good question to illustrate this might be something like "What feels right to you when you're not feeling angry and frustrated?" Such questions show that you're not only trying to help them be true to the organization and to themselves, but to their best selves and to the culture that you share.

This doesn't mean you're there to point out the right thing. Your role is to help them come up with the right thing themselves. Then, you'll give them the encouragement, the authority, and the responsibility to do it. You help most by getting people to look within themselves for answers and by providing an encouraging, accepting, and nonjudgmental atmosphere. You do this best by actively listening (we'll say more about this later), by empathizing, and by giving encouragement and authority to deal with the problem effectively.

Not every interview, of course, will be to deal with problems. Often, you'll want to have interviews to get better acquainted, to see what support is needed, to help someone set goals, or to keep yourself quietly informed. It's often a good idea to have regular interviews in which you let the other person set most of the agenda. Make it their time and give them considerable latitude to discuss the things that are important to them. Use the time to give specific and positive feedback on their work. Also, encourage them to tell you positive things about others in the organization so that together you can maintain high expectations.

Effective Communications.

A CEO for a large corporation decided that he needed better communications with his employees. So, once a year, he visited each of the plant locations and assembled all the employees to talk to them about the progress of the company and how their work helped the company. Then he would open up the floor for questions and discussion, with many comments and questions usually forthcoming.

He was shocked, then, when a year later, shortly after his tour, a damaging strike was called by the hourly workers. He could not understand why none of the issues raised by the strike had even been mentioned in his yearly sessions with employees. A consultant, Russell Ackoff, pointed out that these sessions were one-sided, allowing him to communicate with employees, but were poorly designed for them to communicate with him. "Why?" the CEO asked. "They were free to raise any issues they chose." Ackoff replied, "When you call the meeting and make a formal presentation, they tend to ask the questions they think you want, especially if they respect you. Would a parishioner publicly ask embarrassing questions of a minister after he had completed a sermon? If you want to hear what they are really thinking, you will need to have a meeting where they make the presentation and you listen and ask questions." When he did so, his relationships throughout the company improved dramatically.[12]

Like this CEO, most managers are shocked if someone tells them they have poor communications with workers. Many feel that getting out occasionally "among the troops," or announcing an "open-door policy" gives them good communications. Nothing could be further from the truth. According to a Newsweek report on August 12, 1996, the most common complaint of American workers was that management does a poor job of communicating with workers.

The basic purpose of good communications is to connect—to share something in common. Indeed, the root meaning of the word "communication" is "to establish something in common." The common element most needed in good communications is a shared understanding.

This requires, however, much more than knowing what words mean. Indeed, only 40 percent of the meaning of most communications comes from the words themselves. Almost 50 percent of meaning comes from nonverbal cues (like facial expression, hand movement, body language, tone of voice, etc.). You can demonstrate that with a simple experiment. Repeat aloud eight times the sentence "I didn't say you have a teaching problem," each time emphasizing a different word. Each of these eight expressions will communicate something very different.[13]

Good communications come about only by actively encouraging accessibility, developing important skills, and being willing to practice basic skills. If you, like the CEO mentioned above, find yourself surprised by employee complaints, chances are your communications need some adjustments. But the payoff of good communications goes far beyond avoiding strikes or constant gripes. The most important benefit is the resulting creativity, energy, and feelings of ownership it produces among your staff.

Perhaps the most important communication skill is *effective listening*. This, of course, is much more than not interrupting while another person speaks. It also involves keeping your mind focused, being able to ask key questions, being able to read body language, and being open-minded and understanding. Among these, staying focused on what the speaker is saying is one of the most difficult. Most people are capable of listening to 600 words per minute, while most of us speak at only about 125 words per minute. This discrepancy leads to the tendency for our minds to wander. We start planning what to say next, and cease paying attention. It is far better to use the "free time" to mentally repeat or summarize what the speaker is saying.

We also need to discipline our minds to pay particular attention right up to the last sentence. Research shows that the last sentence or two usually contain the most essential information. Speakers often wait until the end of their utterance to make key points or to clarify their discussion. Unfortunately, that's usually when most of us are preparing our own response, thus missing the most essential elements of what they have to say.

One technique that enhances both listening and communication is to briefly summarize what the other person has said (introduced in Chapter Four). If you do, state what you are doing and why—to make certain you have correctly understood. When you know you will summarize, you will most likely pay close attention to what is being said so that you do not misrepresent it. It also lets you be sure that you have really understood what the other person is saying. In addition, it gives the other person the chance to clarify their message. Finally, it communicates that you really care enough about what he is saying to want to get it right.

A closely-related skill is to reflect feelings, or attempt to describe not only what the person said, but the feelings he or she seemed to convey (with tone, body language, facial expressions, etc.). This skill, of course, requires an ability to discern what someone is feeling, and to listen with empathy. This skill is especially important in listening to someone from a different generation, ethnic group, or gender than your own.

Empathetic listening[14] to pick up on feelings is the highest level of skill in effective listening. Below it, in descending order of listening states, are **attentive listening** (paying close attention to what is said), **selective listening** (hearing only those parts of what is said that interest us), **pretended listening** (giving only the appearance of listening), and **complete inattention**. Empathetic listening can pay big dividends, but it is difficult for many executives, especially those who are more transactional, rather than transformational, leaders. Transactional leaders want to fix problems, so they listen only long enough to diagnose a problem and then begin to prescribe its solution. Transformational leaders, on the other hand, are more interested in building people, so they tend to listen, not only to content, but to feelings.

Often, when someone is saying something with which we disagree, it is tempting to jump in and indicate our disagreement. In many teams, this violates a basic ground rule of not interrupting when someone is speaking. Teams that support this ground rule often make it clear that listening carefully and even asking clarifying questions, should not be taken as signs of agreement. Thus, a person is allowed to make her point, and even have it clarified, before others indicate whether they agree or disagree.

Another skill of effective communications is to develop the ability to clearly state your points and offer supporting information. One of the most helpful ways of doing this is to prepare yourself so that you know what you want people to understand. If you are preparing a speech, for example, try organizing your presentation around concepts, rather than topics. A concept is an idea, generally expressed as a complete sentence. For example, rather than saying "I will talk about. . . .(a topic--e.g., our budget problems)," try finishing this sentence, "I want them to understand that. . . .(a concept–e.g., we have overspent our budget and need to cut back)." Basing your presentations on concepts forces you to organize your ideas in a meaningful sequence. You can then prepare supporting concepts and examples for each of your key concepts.

Negotiation and Conflict Resolution.

One evening, Linda Lantieri was walking down a desolate, dangerous block lined with abandoned, boarded-up buildings when suddenly, out of nowhere, she was surrounded by three boys about fourteen years old. One pulled out a knife with a four-inch blade as they pressed in around her. "Give me your purse! Now!" the boy with the knife hissed. Though frightened, Lantieri had the presence of mind to take some deep breaths and reply coolly, "I'm feeling a little uncomfortable. You know, guys, you're a little into my space. I'm wondering if you could step back a little." Lantieri studied the sidewalk and, to her amazement, she saw three pairs of sneakers take a few steps back. "Thank you," she said, then continued, "Now, I want to hear what you just said to me, but to tell you the truth, I'm a little nervous about that knife. I'm wondering if you could put it away."

After what seemed an eternity of silence and uncertainty, the knife went back into a pocket.

Quickly reaching into her purse, Lantieri took out a $20 bill, caught the eye of the one with the knife, and asked, "Who should I give it to?"

"Me," he said.

Glancing at the other two, she asked if they agreed. One of the two nodded.

"Great," she said, handing the leader the $20 bill. "Now here's what's going to happen. I'm going to stay right here while you walk away."

With puzzled looks on their faces, the boys slowly started to walk away, glancing over their shoulders at Lantieri and then they broke into a run. They were running from her![15]

Lantieri´s amazing presence of mind in this situation is no minor accomplishment. She is the founder and director of the Resolving Conflict Creatively Program, which teaches negotiation skills in schools. She learned the skills of negotiation and handling conflict amicably while working as a teacher in a Harlem school, not far from where this incident took place. She now has training programs in more than four hundred schools throughout the United States.

Fortunately, most conflict situations are seldom as extreme as the one just described. Still, all of us face some form of conflict virtually every day. In fact, when your team really comes to feel deeply about the cause and your mission, conflict may occur more frequently.[16] This is because conflict is most likely to occur when people have strong feelings about something. Knowing how to handle conflict situations is a vital part of managing an effective early childhood center.

At the heart of successful conflict resolution is the application of the principles discussed earlier. When someone comes to you with a major conflict, for example, put it in its proper context. When viewed alongside our shared sense of cause and our shared vision, most conflicts will fade in size, and thus become more manageable.[17] We also need to help conflicting individuals accept ownership for their problems, and we express our expectations for courageous and unselfish solutions to these problems. Finally, we work for win-win solutions, rather than letting disputes degenerate into fights over who will win and who will lose.

This last principle is particularly important in conflict resolution. People will often come to you with a conflict in which they insist upon a particular position. Rather than taking your own position and then negotiating, it is far better to take the time to find out what each party's interests or needs are.

One side might say, for example, that they want a particular resource or concession. Through a series of questions, you can generally find out what they really need, or what their main interests are. Once you know these needs, you can then seek for a solution that will help them meet these needs, even though they do not get what they were demanding when they stated their position.

Box 6.1 Conflict
Conflict is "...a sign of a healthy organization—but only up to a point. A good manager doesn't try to eliminate conflict; he tries to keep it from wasting the energies of his people.
Conviction is a flame that must burn--in trying an idea or fighting for a chance to try it. If bottled up inside, it will eat a person's heart away.
If you're the boss and your people fight you openly when they think you're wrong--that's healthy. If your people fight each other openly in your presence for what they believe in - that's healthy. But keep all the conflicts eyeball to eyeball.
--Robert Townsend, 1984

One of the obstacles that frequently keeps people from win-win solutions is the anger or intense feelings that often accompany conflicts. Anger and deep-seated resentment drive individuals towards trying to win at someone else's expense. So, a first step in conflict resolution is to calm people down. After everyone has their emotions in check, you may want to let them acknowledge, or even express, their feelings but never in cutting or accusatory ways. Often, you may need to establish (or remind people of) some basic ground rules. For example, you may insist that everyone state their point of view in neutral language rather than using argumentative or provocative statements. You may also insist that people not use emotion-laden words and that they stick to facts.

If people are unable to calm down immediately, or if any of you are rushed, you may wish to postpone the conflict-resolution session to a better time and place (though you should make sure this is agreeable to everyone). If the conflict is a "showstopper," however, handle it immediately, putting everything else on hold.

When you are ready to proceed, get everyone to indicate their willingness to resolve the issue by talking it out, rather than letting it escalate with more hostility or aggression. If it starts to escalate, or if you perceive that people are not really listening to or understanding, each other, ask each side to summarize their understanding of what the other is saying. It is amazing how often disputes occur because people have quit listening or have misunderstood what the other side is saying.

The best solutions will surface as you get each side to discuss ideas that will meet their own needs and those of the other party. Together, you must then select one of these proposed solutions (or a combination of several) that all can agree upon. Strive for consensus, or an agreement that everyone can live with. Also, make sure that all parties willingly acknowledge their support for the decision. Don't stop until you have worked out all relevant details, such as who will do what, by when, and other such decisions. Finally, if there is a possibility of misconception, indicate that you will draft a memo that outlines your understanding of the agreement. Then, forward this to each party and ask for some form of acknowledgement or clarification. Do not leave the session, however, until you have expressed your appreciation to all parties for their willingness to find a solution that works for the good of the organization and of each party.

Effective Discipline through Accountability.

The Texas Department of Mental Health and Mental Retardation had a serious problem. Employee turnover and absenteeism rates among its 26,000 employees were very high, which affected not only the morale but also the well-being of patients. To make matters worse, these problems turned into labor disputes. It became increasingly clear that an antagonistic relationship had developed between management and the workers. After implementing a "Discipline Without Punishment" approach, however, the turnover rate fell by 30 percent in the first quarter alone, saving the agency 1.7 million dollars per quarter in training and replacement costs.[18]

The heart of the problem for this agency was its antiquated system of punishing employee behavior. Under the old boss-style management common in many organizations, bad behavior was formally punished. This approach is based on the assumption that, unless clear punishment is given, workers will think managers are weak, leading to even worse behavior. In addition to the fears about losing control, many bosses support punishment because it's the way they were raised. If you don't punish misbehavior, they believe, everyone will start doing it.

In recent years, many organizations like the Texas Department of Mental Health and Mental Retardation have discovered that discipline works far better than punishment. Discipline, as we pointed out earlier, is what we do for someone, while punishment is what we do to someone. This is much more than just a play on words. The basic assumption of discipline is that people will behave responsibly with appropriate guidance. Discipline is also based on establishing a collaborative relationship. Both management and workers want to accomplish the same thing. With discipline, you also maintain high expectations for positive behavior.

Punishment, on the other hand, assumes a basic mistrust of those who misbehave. In addition, it frequently leads us to hold ever-lower expectations of them and leads to an "us-versus-them" mentality. Punished individuals are not just at odds with management. They want to save face with fellow employees and will recruit allies to support their feeling of being unfairly treated. As a result, punished individuals must often be given even stronger penalties, generally leading to sabotage and/or their eventual termination.

The basic problem of punishment-oriented systems is seen in a simple truth. People will not become better if we treat them progressively worse. Punishment may work in the short term, but it often produces a host of negative "side effects." In addition, punishment reduces the chance that most people will internalize basic values and beliefs, thus damaging a powerful form of motivation. Discipline is the only policy consistent with team leadership. Punishment not only makes you "the heavy," but it flies in the face of the principles of empowerment. You can't empower people and then try to control them with punishment. If your system of dealing with employee misbehavior is punishment-oriented, it's time for a change.

The following story illustrates the effective use of discipline by one early childhood center director.

> One of my teachers came to work dressed very inappropriately. I sent her home, telling her to change and that I would not dock her pay. She got an attitude. " If I go home," she said, " I will stay home." I said, "Do what you have to do. Just fill out a sick-day form and stay home." About 10 minutes later she called from her car and said, "You were right. I was not appropriately dressed, and I will change and come back." She explained that she was really upset with a staff member, and not at me, because of what that person had said about her dress for the day. I said, "That's all right. So just change and come back." When she came back, I told her that I appreciated her doing the professional thing. I don't really discipline; I just redirect. If I think someone is trying to be workable, I will work with them.

What are the basic elements of a system that puts discipline in place of punishment? The core principle is the idea that individuals should be held responsible to make sound choices, with appropriate support. Further, it shifts the burden of making changes from the leader to the employee. In effect, employees are asked to discipline themselves, with our support and encouragement. This will become clear in the end-of-chapter exercise to examine some of the steps of one disciplinary system designed by John Huberman.[19]

Delegation.

Many leaders fail to see delegation as a skill. They see it as simply transferring a portion of their responsibility to someone else. This way of looking at delegation can be dangerous because such leaders will probably fail to transfer a full sense of ownership along with the responsibility. True delegation requires not only the effective transfer of responsibility, but of ownership, information, authority, and of the trust that will be needed to get the job done well.

Transactional leaders are often reluctant to delegate. In many cases, they are more concerned about getting the job done than building the person to whom the assignment is delegated. They may prefer to do the job themselves, either because they want it done their way, or because they don't want to spend the time teaching and training someone else to do it. A transformational leader, on the other hand, frequently delegates an assignment that would be easier to do herself because she wants to give someone else an opportunity to grow. Delegation develops other people by giving them the chance to take additional responsibility, learn new skills, build their confidence, and stretch their initiative.

In reality, delegation is an investment in getting work done well, as well as in other people. Once you teach people to take ownership, as well as the responsibility delegated, you will duplicate yourself and multiply your efforts immensely. In order to delegate effectively, you will need to see the potential in people and help them take responsibility that will bring out qualities that they may not yet see in themselves.

Effective delegation also requires you to take some serious thought about the assignment you are delegating. Are you willing to clearly communicate your expectations about the assignment? This would include being clear about desired outcomes, resources available, applicable rules, and where they can go for help. Are you truly willing to give them authority to make necessary decisions? You will never transfer ownership unless you are willing to transfer the authority to make decisions without coming to you about every detail.

When you delegate a responsibility, be sure to delegate the assignment, not the methods, or you will be guilty of micro-managing. You have to give people some room to make decisions, even if that means living with having the task done differently than you would do it. This willingness is illustrated in the following case study.

> An Early Head Start director experienced constant headaches and complaining about how meals were served. So she called in her staff and gave them responsibility to solve the problem. One of the issues was about how to dispose of food. "I do not like the way they are doing the milk right now," she says. "It really bothers me to see them pour all that unused milk into a large container. It looked terrible. The kids were pouring their leftover milk into a large, clear bucket. It reminded me of pig slop. I mentioned it to them, but left the decision up to them. So, they changed the containers from clear to black." Now, the director still may not like it, but she cannot pull back the authority for making the decision without taking away the

ownership they feel for finding solutions. The constant bickering is gone, and everyone is searching for workable solutions. Accepting something different from her own preference is a small price to pay for the ownership they now feel.

As Box 6.2[20] indicates effective delegation does not happen overnight. You have to recognize where people are in their commitment and in their competence, and then help them develop each by taking on increasingly larger assignments. Whenever you delegate these assignments, however, it is absolutely essential that you clearly communicate: 1) desired outcomes; 2) what authority you are giving them; 3) resources they will have available; 4) how and when they can report accomplishments

Box 6.2

About my fourth year (as superintendent), I realized that I would never be able to accomplish significant change by myself. I needed to pay more attention to relationships with the community, the School Board, and the teachers. The union leadership and I agreed, for example, on a contract but the membership voted it down. The School Board and the community saw me as an arrogant stranger from New York. I had recognized that I needed other people to make change happen, but now I realized that I could not be their teacher. We were all learners together.

or problems; and 5) any special rules or guidelines (written or only understood) that both of you will have to live with.

Integrating Skills and Principles into Improved Relationships.

Though these and other factors are extremely important in producing effective leaders, it is the merging of skills and principles that enhances that process. Leadership in today's world is increasingly less about power and more about applying correct principles and skills. Like the superintendent in the story above Box 6.2 those who fail to integrate the two components, principles and skills, will win some battles only to find they are losing the war.[21]

Chapter Application Exercises
I. Personal Reflection Exercise

It is difficult for most people in supervisory positions to see their mistakes in handling relationships. Partly, this is because people may be afraid to say anything. But it may also be the result of self-deception. It is easy when a person has power to think the problem lies with others, rather than with herself. Carefully consider the following questions to determine how well you handle relationships.

1. Do you make people feel a sense of belonging-that they are needed and worthwhile, or do you frequently just say things to make them feel worthwhile, not really believing it?

2. Is your communication with people more to bless, or to impress?

3. As you interact with people for whom you are responsible, are you more interested in getting them to do their jobs or in helping them develop their potential?

4. Do you conduct interviews in an unhurried manner? Do you spend most of the time talking, or listening? Do you direct the conversation most of the time, or do you let the other person determine what issues will be discussed?

5. Do you listen empathetically? Do you find yourself listening attentively? How often do you interrupt or cut people off?

Identify two or three settings in which your communication is especially critical to your leadership success (in meetings, one-on-one, etc.). Over the next two weeks, keep a simple journal on your own communication. Identify two things that seem to go well and two things that you would like to change.

Group Exercises
A. Effective Listening

Pair up with another person. One of you will begin to speak about a topic of current interest (for example, how you have been affected by terrorism). The other person will listen carefully, without saying anything. After a minute or so, the listener will take a turn, but to do so must say, "Let me see if I have understood you correctly." Then describe, as closely as you can, what the first speaker has been saying. If this summary is accurate, the first speaker will say, "Yes, that is what is meant." If something is incorrect, or a major element of the communication has been left out, the first speaker will say instead, "No, I must not have been clear. What I said was (repeating the missing or misunderstood element)." After the listener gets it right, the first speaker will listen while the first listener speaks, with the same summarization sequence at the end. Now repeat the exercise, this time listening emphatically. Repeat not only what you think the other person said, but reflect what you understand the other person was feeling. You might say something like, "I'm picking up that you feel ...."

After each of you have had an opportunity so speak and to listen empathetically, accurately summarizing the other person's total communication, discuss how you were affected by this exercise. For example, did you listen differently? Did you find yourself not paying attention at any point? If so why? Finally, try listening emphatically to a child, attempting to repeat not only content, but feelings. If you have an opportunity, report your experience back to the group.

B. Discipline vs. Punishment

Read the following description of an effective discipline program developed for industry. Then, meet in groups to discuss what elements could be adapted to your organization's discipline program.

Discipline vs. Punishment--The Huberman Model

With the first occurrence of employee misbehavior, an informal "oral reminder" is presented. This reminder, discussed in a private meeting, is designed to encourage the employee to accept responsibility for solving the problem. This discussion is not a warning. It is, however, an attempt to help the employee understand his or her personal responsibility to meet reasonable standards of performance and behavior. In this meeting, you mention that a summary of the conversation (and your agreement) will be placed in a working file, but that no official record will go into his or her personal file.

If the problem recurs, the next step is a written reminder and another private discussion. Again, no threats are made. You attempt to work out an agreement on what the employee pledges to do to solve the problem. This time, a memo of the conversation is sent to the employee, and a copy is placed in his or her file. At this stage, the focus shifts from an emphasis on wrong behavior to the failure to keep the previous commitment. Still, it is important to stress your expectation that he/she will abide by his/her agreements and that you will do all you can to help him/her to accomplish that goal.

If the behavior is still not corrected, you move to the third step-a one-day "decision-making leave." The leave is paid to show that the organization is committed to helping resolve the problem. At the same time, you make it very clear that continuation with the organization depends on his/her decision to solve the immediate problem, make a commitment to a total and positive change, and to honor the commitments. Upon return from this leave, disciplined employees do not immediately return to work. Rather, they meet with you to discuss their decision. If they decide to stay, they agree to work with you to formulate a specific action plan. You again express confidence that they will live up to the agreement, but you also emphasize that failure to do so will necessarily lead to termination.

This disciplinary process is characterized by a good-faith effort to help the individual perform up to his capability and to accept responsibility. It also puts you on the same side with employees and gives responsibility for correcting misbehavior where it belongs-on the misbehaving individual. As a result, it not only improves employee morale, but also puts you in a strong legal position if termination ever becomes necessary.

Some people are concerned that disciplinary systems such as this might excuse bad behavior. In response, we emphasize that understanding should not be confused with excusing. People are still held accountable for their behavior. In fact, they are made even more accountable because the burden for correcting misbehavior is shifted from the supervisor to the offending employee.

Some managers dislike the idea of a paid leave, believing that it will reward bad behavior. Managers who have used the system say there is no need to worry. Employees who have been on the receiving end of a paid disciplinary leave agree. One employee, given a one-day suspension commented, "Believe me, brother, that was no vacation."

In contrast, those given an unpaid leave or suspension often come back to work feeling bitter, embarrassed, and angry. In addition, they come back feeling they've already paid their dues and owe the company nothing. Said one supervisor, "I've never seen a guy come back from an unpaid suspension feeling better about his boss, his job, the company, or himself."

Additional Instructions: This exercise is best handled with a facilitator chosen from your team. Maximize participation so that all team members contribute to the discussion. If there is more than one group, have them all get back together and reach consensus about how this model could be instituted in your organization.

Chapter Notes

1 This is a study by Jean B. Leslie and Ellen Van Velsor, cited in Daniel Goleman, *Working with Emotional Intelligence* (New York: Bantam Books, 1998), 40.

2 Goleman, *Working with Emotional Intelligence*, 40, 41.

3 Goleman, *Working with Emotional Intelligence*, 13.

4 Goleman, *Working with Emotional Intelligence*, 317.

5 Goleman, *Working with Emotional Intelligence*, 7.

6 Goleman, *Working with Emotional Intelligence*, 4.

7 Dean K. Whitla, "Value added: Measuring the Impact of Undergraduate Education," (Office of Instructional Research and Evaluation, Harvard University, 1975).

8 For an excellent discussion of using principles in management, see Stephen R. Covey, *Principle-Centered Leadership*.

9 Covey, *Principle-Centered Leadership*, 192.

10 Goleman, *Working with Emotional Intelligence*, 149-150.

11 Duncan and Pinegar, *Leadership for Saints*, 177.

12 From Russel L. Ackoff, *Ackoff's Best: His Classic Writings on Management*, (New York: John Wiley and Sons, Inc., 1999) 182-183.

13 This example, and the discussion of the meaning of the word "communication," is based on an insightful discussion of the subject by Duncan and Pinegar, *Leadership for Saints*, 165-167.

14 This, and the other forms of listening, are adapted from a discussion by Duncan and Pinegar, *Leadership for Saints*, 171, 172.

15 From Goleman, *Working with Emotional Intelligence*, 181, 182.

16 As Box 6.1 shows, conflict can have positive results. Based on Robert Townsend, *Further Up the Organization* (New York: Knopf, 1984).

17 In a well known Bible story, King Solomon used this principle when he informed two mothers fighting over a baby that he would cut the baby in half. The woman who saw the baby's well-being as more important than winning a custody battle was judged to be the child's true mother.

18 Based on Jonathan King and Robert E. Johnson, "Silk Purses From Old Plants" in *Harvard Business Review*, April 1983, 147.

19 The one we describe here is one based on a system developed by John Huberman, as described in the Harvard Business Review, July - August, 1985, 162-177.

20 Based on Peter Negroni, "The Superintendent's Progress" in Peter Senge (Ed.). *Schools That Learn*, (New York: Doubleday, 2000) 425-432

21 Adapted from The Superintendent's Progress: Moving from "Lone Ranger" to Lead Learner in an Urban School System, in Peter Senge (Ed.). *Schools That Learn*, (New York: Doubleday, 2000) 425 - 432.

Chapter Seven.
"In It for the Long Haul."
Conducting Effective Team Training and Team Support Against Burnout

Chapter Summary

A good training program requires you to change old habits, develop organizational culture, and build effective relationships. It also calls for you to develop an on-going assessment strategy, select training modules, provide extensive practice opportunities, and set up realistic feedback mechanisms. Training and staff development can help avoid burnout by providing strong team support. Everyone must work hard to keep the mission and sense of cause always in clear view of team members. Establishing appropriate boundaries also allows you to give your best during work hours without taking problems home with you.

Training people to work as a team is hard work. One outstanding advocate of team leadership works with organizations and individuals who respond enthusiastically to the principles and skills that he teaches. Then, he gets them to do role playing. Almost without exception, the team leader will say something like, "This is the problem, and this is what I feel we should do about it." Then, he or she makes assignments to team members. While this might be a good exercise in delegation, it fails to bring out the experience and wisdom of team members. So, he suggests to the team leader that he or she try again, this time getting ideas and recommendations from team members (especially from those who are less inclined to participate). It's hard for many leaders to break old habits, but those who do experience very positive results.[1]

Introduction

Everything we have discussed in the preceding chapters will take time and real effort to put into practice. It's a long-term commitment, but it will pay off both shortly and in the more distant future. You will need to set up a training system that consists of much more than consultants giving one-day seminars. You will also need to find ways to handle changes as they become necessary. Finally, there is also much that you can and should do to reduce the pressures that lead to burnout. If you will make up your mind to do it right, making these changes will be a rewarding experience for everyone, and a great benefit to the families that depend on you.

Effective Staff Development

A Training Consultant Says: It was the staff development day from Hell. Even though we started "fresh" in the morning, most of the participants came to the session stressed and worn out. As they came in and sat down, it was clear that there were several "loners" in the group, as well as definite "cliques." A lot of conflict was just below the surface, even though they knew enough to keep quiet about it in the presence of me, the outsider.

As I began the session, it was clear that the participants had had no input into the content that I had been asked to teach. They were attending because someone said they had to. Their comments revealed that little planning had gone on as to what staff development was really needed, or what the participants wanted. Worse, there was virtually no carry-over from one session to the next. In addition, they had no chance to practice what they had been taught, and even less opportunity to implement it with meaningful feedback. Worse still, no program administrators were present for the training. I had told the director that the changes I would be presenting had to have full support and understanding from the top, as well as from the teachers and competency experts who were expected to put it all into practice.

Things didn't get much better as the day went on. I was able to entertain them, and even received a very high evaluation on the "popularity scale" they filled out at the end of the session. Still, I went away knowing that nothing I had taught that day would be implemented in any meaningful way.

It would be nice if such experiences were rare. Unfortunately, much of the staff development and training that takes place in organizations, both large and small, public as well as private, is little different from that described above. All of us have had to sit through training that, while sometimes entertaining (and often not!) is of little long-term value. Daniel Goleman[2] calls it the "billion-dollar mistake," wasting precious resources on training programs that have little lasting impact.

Goleman cites a study done in 1996 by the American Society

for Training and Development that revealed that only 13 percent of companies actually evaluated their training to see how it affected on-the-job performance. As one executive put it, we "spray and pray-expose everybody to the training and hope it sticks to some." A year later, ASTD did another study of 35 highly-esteemed companies. This study revealed that only two-thirds made any attempt to evaluate their training. Most of those who did relied on such soft measures as how much their employees liked the training. Almost none attempted to see how training actually affected job performance. Another 1997 study on the effect of training to develop interpersonal capabilities among managers found that several programs were utterly worthless, including one five-day mountain retreat to teach executives the skills of team building.

Of course, many training programs are extremely valuable. Five leadership programs evaluated in the same study, for example, showed a return on investment in the first year as high as 492 percent. One very successful program paid for itself in only three weeks and gave a 2000 percent return by the end of the first year.

The problem with most training, however, is that no one bothers to investigate whether it has had the desired effect. Most evaluations consist of popularity measures that ask participants to say how much they liked the training. Such evaluations tend to reward the slick, fun experiences over those that require a lot of tough hard work. As Goleman concludes, "Having a good time becomes the mark of excellence, a value of entertainment over education."[3]

Staff development is essential to the implementation of successful team management. You will have to devote considerable effort to it so that everyone becomes proficient in the skills and committed to the principles. A good staff development day is just the beginning. You have to build in practice and feedback. You must also follow up from one training session to the next, integrating each element of staff development with those that follow. We are talking about changing organizational culture and individual habits, not just adding a skill or two.

Much learning is indirect. For example, as you and your co-workers labor together to define your cause, you develop many of the skills of team leadership. Thus, most learning takes place, not in training sessions, but as you incorporate skills and principles in your daily work. Training sessions can show how to do something, may even help people understand why it needs doing. Actually learning to do it, though, and making it a habit, or part of your organizational culture, takes place only with considerable practice and when feedback exchanged among team members.

Your greatest gains, therefore, will not be made with occasional staff development days. They only supplement real staff development.

Edward T. Joyner, (see Box 7.1) calls our over-reliance on training days "drive-by staff development."[4] This term includes all training that fails to pre-assess individual and organizational needs and that fails to integrate staff development with long-range planning. You must match the training to the needs identified in your strategic planning.

Pre-assessment should also measure the readiness of different individuals for particular training needs. Much of the resistance to training is directed at the "one-size-fits-all" approach that assumes each person is equally ready, or equally needy. If one or two people lack a particular skill, don't subject those who already possess it to unnecessary training. Let those who possess the skill help those who are learning it.

This leads us

Box 7.1

At Bowling Park Elementary School in Norfolk, Virginia, a custodian concerned about the way some sixth-grade boys were behaving got the principal's permission to involve the boys in landscaping around the school. For a little bit of money, the boys worked with him on weekends. After lunch, he would talk to them about a wide variety of issues. Before long, their grades went up, and the teachers noticed a marked difference in their behavior. The custodian couldn't teach them academic skills, but he was highly effective at helping them with their social and ethical development. He also taught them that work, no matter what kind of work, has an innate dignity. When the principal received a national leadership award, the custodian was on the podium with him.

---

to the idea of supplementing your training with models. Those who have mastered a skill become models for those who are just learning it. In fact, some organizations try to make each employee a model of at least one skill. Even your cooks and your custodians can be models, as the accompanying box story illustrates. We believe the idea of using models has advantages over that of using "mentors." Making everyone a model for some skill teaches that each individual can be very good at something. Designating a few select individuals as mentors, in contrast, may erroneously convey the idea that a few child care professionals are superior in all important teaching areas.

The team approach to staff development emphasizes training of members by each other. Outside consultants, or trainers, can be a useful resource, but it is a mistake to rely too heavily on them. Generally, outside consultants don't know your team members and your unique situation. Because they are here today and gone tomorrow, they generally have much less commitment to make the training work. Thus, though they can be an important part of your staff development, you should not rely on them for bringing about the most fundamental of changes.

Outsiders can be valuable in some specialized ways. While you are attempting to learn some of the skills we have discussed (strategic planning, for example), a well-trained outsider can model the skills so that team members can then learn to use them also. Likewise, on some occasions you may wish to have an outsider facilitate a process so team members can pay attention to the outcome, without having to worry about running the process. The outsider may enjoy an advantage in conducting a needs assessment, since people often open up to a trusted outsider who will not be around to share secrets. All of these uses of an outsider supplement your own work together in staff development, but they do not replace it.

Support for effective staff development must come from all levels of your organization if you want to successfully make the change to effective team leadership. This support must include a safe environment for experimentation. Most individuals are unwilling to try something new if they believe their first efforts will be harshly evaluated. At the same time, people need recognition for their efforts. Make sure that you show recognition in ways that matter to the individual and to the team.

Team Support Against Burnout

Team management not only eases staff development, but helps prevent burnout. In very broad terms, burnout can be defined as feeling very seriously stressed and unable to cope with the pressures of one's work. Some observers see employee burnout as the number-one threat to early childhood professionals. This danger is illustrated by the following account from one Early Head Start Center.

> A few years ago, we had a young woman come to work for us who loved working with children. She just naturally knew what to do with infants. She was really motivated to organize the classroom to help each baby and his or her family. But back then, we had 12 infants and only two teachers. All of the parents wanted her to hold their child most of the time or otherwise care for their child like there were no other infants around. To make matters worse, our administration was demanding all kinds of paperwork and reports. She started getting really negative, finding fault with everyone and everything. Then she started calling in sick a lot. She finally just quit. Even though she got a better-paying job somewhere else, she lost the opportunity to work with children, and we lost a very good teacher.[5]

Cases like this are all too common in early childhood centers. Though children may sometimes be a source of stress, it is the other demands-the constant paperwork, an upcoming evaluation, demanding or uncooperative parents, and all the bureaucratic red tape that tend to drive most childcare workers crazy. On top of this, many individuals who work with children face additional frustrations in their personal lives, in part because the work they do is often under-appreciated and poorly paid.

All of this can be handled if team members support each other. This does not just mean providing moral support. Though a pat on the back and a shoulder to cry on might be important, childcare professionals need other forms of support to avoid burnout. You may recall a story in Chapter Five about researchers who found that some hardy executives could handle almost any stress, personal, bureaucratic, or otherwise, and still keep their cool. Researchers found that the difference between these hardy executives and those who burned out was the strong sense of mission, or cause, these executives possessed.

One of America's foremost biographers, Studs Terkel, found that a deep sense of commitment to something really important can carry individuals through the hardest of times. Terkel interviewed hundreds of people from many walks of life. His interviews revealed that the individuals most able to resist burnout were those who felt a deep sense of mission. In his book *Working:* People Talk about What They Do All Day And How They Feel About It,[6] Studs Terkel reported that people who work in the helping professions (schools, medicine, social work, etc.) have to endure enormous frustrations and stress. Those best able to cope believe that their work has a higher purpose than putting food on the table. They feel they are part of a very important cause, and it keeps them going even when their work is frustrating and tough.

But feeling committed to an important cause is not enough. In fact, strongly committed people may be at greater risk of burnout if they feel constantly frustrated in accomplishing their cause. Dr. Herbert Freudenberger, the person who coined the term *burnout* called it "a state of fatigue *brought on by devotion to a cause,* a way of life, or a relationship that fails to produce the expected reward (emphasis added)." While a sense of cause is important in preventing burnout, something else is needed.

You may recall that the hardy executives in the research just mentioned also had something else that helped them keep going against killer stress. They also had a strong feeling of being in control of their work and of their lives. The teacher of infants in the story described above had a strong sense of cause, but felt frustrated by expectations she could not fulfill and the overwhelming bureaucratic restrictions. Her burnout was predictable because, though deeply committed, she had little control over her work and felt unable to accomplish what she needed.

The need of highly-motivated people to have considerable control over their work reminds us of documented cases of airline pilots who fly airplanes in spite of a fear of heights. As long as these pilots are able to actually control the aircraft, they are not bothered by their fear.

They report much greater difficulty, however, when they have to ride as passengers on these same aircraft. In the same way, strongly committed workers can effectively resist burnout if they have sufficient control over their work. Burnout, then, can be significantly reduced by two elements of team management: a strong sense of cause and empowerment (which gives team members at all levels a greater sense of control over their work).

The teacher in the preceding story needed team members to help her hang on to the sense of cause. She also needed leaders who would empower her and other team members to solve problems and make team decisions--giving them greater control over their work. Worker empowerment, along with team support and a deep sense of cause, are powerful antidotes to burnout.

Let's look a little more closely at what burnout is. Cathy Willis calls it "a debilitating psychological condition brought about by unrelieved work stress which results in deleted energy reserves, lowered resistance to illnesses, increased dissatisfaction and pessimism, and increased absenteeism and inefficiency at work." For some, burnout brings a sense of diminished personal accomplishment, or feeling that you are doing your job poorly. For some, it results in caving in to the pessimistic belief that the job is not worth doing well at all.

Not everyone experiences burnout in the same way. For most, is comes on slowly. Early symptoms include a feeling of emotional and physical exhaustion; a sense of alienation, cynicism, impatience, negativism, and feelings of detachment, to the point of resenting work and the people one is supposed to help. A formerly deeply-caring person may become emotionally detached, no longer caring at all. Some research suggests that women are a bit more likely to experience emotional exhaustion, while men might more often experience withdrawal and an "I don't care anymore" cynicism. Physical symptoms might include low energy and chronic fatigue, nagging colds and frequent illnesses, frequent headaches, nausea, muscle tension, changes in eating habits, difficulties sleeping, and even shortness of breath.

Burnout is frequently accompanied by a loss of self-esteem, absenteeism, and frequent tardiness. Individuals experiencing it feel they are working more to accomplish less. Many begin to find fault with clients, colleagues, or management, and seem to be chronically disappointed and unenthusiastic. For some, burnout leads to social withdrawal or isolation, feeling that your body is letting you down, and denial of what body, mind, and spirit are saying. In many cases, burnout on the job spills over into family and personal relationships, creating a vicious downward spiral as relationships increasingly deteriorate.

A variety of reasons have been proposed to explain why burnout is more common in the helping professions. Some of it can be explained by the nature of our work with people whose lives are frequently in trouble. Many of us only see the problem side of these people because it's the problems that often bring them to us. Some resist our help, or become resentful of having to depend on us. In addition, many of the helping professions are poorly paid and are misunderstood by the general public. To make matters worse, many helping professionals seldom see the positive outcomes of their work, especially when they have a high caseload or only short-term contact.

Burnout is much more common than many people imagine. In one study of 40,000 people worldwide, 40% were judged to be in one stage or another of burnout. In Japan, 40% of workers were diagnosed as being in the most advanced stages of burnout. These stages include an onset where one's job seems to have become stagnant and where everyday frustrations and minor obstacles seem to become major trials. This is followed by a chronic stage characterized by feelings of powerlessness, apathy, and a self-protective emotional detachment. In the final stage, a person's self esteem, productivity, family relationships, and mental and physical health may seriously deteriorate.

Christina Maslach, one of the foremost experts on burnout, argues that burnout is not just a psychological symptom of work stress, but the result of unmanaged work stress. In her book, *The Truth about Burnout*,[7] she emphasizes that burnout is a management problem that requires management decisions about work relationships and the nature of the workplace. She and her co-author, Michael P. Leiter, propose that burnout requires important changes in on-the-job relationships.

It's easy to miss this point. Most people see burnout as a psychological problem, failing to see its organizational aspects. The lack of a sense of personal mastery, for example, can be seen as a psychological situation. The organization of bureaucracy, however, cuts down on how much mastery an individual actually has. Similarly, alienation and feeling cut off from others is psychological, but organizations that fail to provide team support contribute by forcing individuals to go it alone. Managers must realize that the lack of team support, the failure to empower team members, as well as bureaucratic goal displacement all contribute to burnout.

This perspective is essential as we look for ways to prevent or cure burnout. We need to use both psychological stress management techniques and organizational change to help those at risk for burnout. Some of the principles and skills introduced in the last chapter can reduce burnout. The principle of ownership, for example, leads us to delegate more and to let others take increasing responsibility.

Strategic planning also helps reduce burnout. As you work as a team to set realistic goals and then work together to find the resources to accomplish them, each person feels empowered in a great cause. As you set priorities, you also reduce the pressures of being pulled in too many directions. A clear plan also reduces anxiety from not knowing what is really expected of each worker. When strategic planning is done right, team members will be able to see how their work is meaningful in the overall mission of the organization.

A major source of relief from burnout comes from a strong, positive organizational culture. Your collective mindset should encourage having fun together, working as a team, and providing mutual support. Your organizational culture should also lead you to minimize bureaucratic routines and regulations that frustrate rather than facilitate. Having ground rules that everyone supports also minimizes the uncertainty that contributes to burnout. The following case study of a very frustrated Early Head Start director illustrates the importance of these team supports against burnout.

> We just completed a federal audit. We did really well, with no findings. Two months prior, I find out in a meeting that I have a mentor! Where did that come from?!!! My "mentor" was someone that just barely has a CDA and no knowledge of EHS. To me, that was the ultimate slap in the face. I had no input. A decision was just made. The "mentor" came to me and apologized for being my mentor and told me that she had no idea about EHS. But soon enough, she was trying to be an authority for me.
>
> I have other frustrations with upper administration. We have a family that has been consistently late picking up their child. So, I talked with the parent five or six times, and she just kept coming late. I asked her to call me when she knows she will be late so that I can make arrangements to take care of her child. Then, she came late again, with no call. So I told her she would be dropped from our program if it happened again. The very next day, she does the same thing. So, I told her she could not continue because I couldn't keep paying staff overtime to take care of her child. I had no other choice. She walked out of my office and made one phone call. The very next day, she came back with her child. I had a phone call from the administration office telling me I had to keep her.
>
> Still, I will not let anyone run me away or burn me out. I have refused to work more than is called for. I could work ten/twelve hours a day. But, they said overtime was forbidden unless we had prior permission. How can you get prior permission to work overtime when you do not know when you will have to stay? I will not allow myself to be abused that way, and I will not let my staff be abused that way. My staff and I talked about it. Now, we have substitutes and that solves a lot of the overtime problems.
>
> We have been through "Holy Hell" with upper administration. But, that keeps the staff together. We go to dinner together. We celebrate birthdays and frequently go to lunch together. My staff stands completely behind me when I go to administration.
>
> I love my staff, and I love the children. I love what EHS

stands for. Getting the families on their feet and rolling with life is great, even though it's really tough with the political environment of our agency. I constantly praise my teachers, but it's sincere. I let the staff leave early when they can and even fifteen minutes can make big difference. It just shows that I noticed their efforts and lets them know they are appreciated.

Still I need an outlet. I frequently have to go to our other center to check on things there. That twenty minute drive is really therapeutic. My family is also a great support. When I go home, I leave work at the center.

As this case illustrates, though team support is very important, team members must find other ways to deal with stress. One of these is learning to set appropriate boundaries between work and other parts of one's life. This means that we should respect each other's "off" time, avoiding work-related calls at home except in emergencies. Managers should also avoid excessive overtime requirements. They need to find ways to give breaks, create some element of private space, and respect the need for an occasional break.

At the personal level, each of us needs to more fully develop all the aspects of our lives, including our spiritual, emotional, physical, and social resources. We can develop spiritual resources, for example, no matter what our religious affiliation (or lack of one) by learning to "keep an attitude of gratitude," giving thanks daily to our Creator. Religion and spirituality can also help one keep a strong sense of priorities and understand why the work with children is so important. The spiritual dimension also helps us keep goals and behavior focused on a larger vision of life. It helps us worry less about things we can't change and focus on those that we can. A spiritual community can also provide powerful support when things are not going well.

Efforts to develop our emotional well-being include learning ways to firmly (but politely) say no. Take on what is comfortable and recognize that everyone has times when they should say no. Avoid negative, destructive talk, complaining and negative people. Get counseling from a trusted friend, spiritual advisor, or professional counselor. Talking to someone you trust (without it becoming gossip) also helps, because it influences our ideas, which in turn affects how we feel. In addition, we need to devote time to things that are fun and things that give a sense of accomplishment. Finally, we can recognize that great things come out of small gains, so we become more patient with God and with ourselves.

A major part of developing the physical part of ourselves involves regular physical exercise. This should be something you enjoy; otherwise, you will likely not stick with it. If you decide to lose weight, change your lifestyle (again, to something you can live with); not your diet. Learn to relax without feeling guilty. A number of relaxation and meditation techniques are very good for this. Doing something stimulating and relaxing on a regular basis also helps, such as taking a walk or participating in an active sport. Other than that, get plenty of sleep. And finally, try to always unwind before going to sleep and try to stick to a regular sleep schedule of eight hours sleep per night.

In the area of *social* development, nurture good friendships. Stay in touch with people you can trust and those with whom you can laugh and enjoy yourself. Strengthen family bonds. Learn time management skills and use them, especially to guarantee private time and family time. People who develop strong family bonds are more adept at resisting burnout, even if those ties entail major obligations or responsibilities. Get involved with others who share similar interests, hobbies, and values. In sum, nurture the relations that nurture you.

Perhaps of greatest importance, however, is getting better control of your time. Some of the best advice we have heard is summarized in the following statement. "Rather than prioritize your schedule, you should schedule your priorities."[8] Don't let good things crowd out those that are essential. Neither should you let things that are urgent crowd out those parts of your life that are really important. In practice, this means that things like phone calls wanting an immediate (but non-essential) response crowd out truly pressing problems and things which are both urgent and important. You can best protect yourself by finding ways to put boundaries around yourself when you need to handle these truly important items.

Conclusion

Throughout this book, we have tried to put principles ahead of programs and an underlying philosophy of human relations ahead of management techniques. To the extent that you understand these principles, you should be able to solve a wide variety of situations. Let's illustrate by looking at the principles and the overall philosophy involved in a very successful effort called the Rainmakers that was designed to help low-income families. This project was developed by an elementary school in Miami Beach, Florida where most of the children's parents were undocumented and extremely poor. Most of the children were doing poorly in school. Police sweeps in the area were common and the housing was overcrowded. Repairs were virtually ignored by landlords. A head lice problem among the children had become so serious that many believed the school should be shut down.

With very limited funding, an agency called "Health Learners" hired a social worker as a family advocate. Because she believed in empowering people, she began knocking on doors and asking for parents to serve as consultants to solve the problem. A small group of them, who called themselves the "Lice Busters," got together. They quickly discovered that the problem was more in the housing conditions than in poor hygiene practices. Some families were living in one-room apartments in abandoned buildings with no running water and only mattresses on the floors for their children. Working with the family advocate, they recommended fumigating services and coins for laundry, as well as medicated shampoo. In addition, they started looking for vacuum cleaners to clean the apartments and scissors to cut the children's hair. Finally, they determined they needed a place for the children to do homework.

The family advocate saw the parents as a resource, rather than the problem. Together, they put on a forty-hour training for the parents, mostly mothers, so they could become paraprofessional social service aides, health aides, tutor aides, teacher aides, and resource supports for one another. With a very small grant, some of the mothers were paid $40 per week. They called themselves the "Rain Mothers," and immediately opened an after-school homework club for the children. When it opened, far more children came than anyone expected.

Next, they set about to solve the problem of absenteeism. If a child missed two or three days of school, Rain Mothers visited the child's home to bring the day's homework and to tell the parents, as neighbors, how much the child had been missed. In short time, the school had some of the highest test scores and the lowest absenteeism rate in the system. When a journalist writing about them called them the "Rainmakers," the title stuck.

Next, they tackled the need for social services, but asked the parents what was needed. Rather than asking for Medicaid and other benefit programs, the parents requested Legal Aid and support groups to deal with gender and violence issues. Many wanted real estate support to work with Legal Aid to help those who had been evicted. The Rainmakers also helped parents work with teachers. One teacher commented, "When you look at a kid in the classroom who's problematic, all you see is the problem. But when there's a Rainmaker advocate, we can see the pressures that the kid is having. And we now see the child in a different way.

Rainmaker projects have been copied in other parts of the country, so it's possible to see that the success was not just the result of one or two key individuals. These successes include tough, violent kids who had already been in jail returning wholeheartedly to school and volunteering community service. The basic philosophy in all Rainmaker programs is the same. Train people to care for their own community, create occupational and educational ladders for them, and get out of the way. In one program, drug dependent parents who had resisted professional help responded much better to Rainmakers who were themselves recovering addicts.

The Rainmakers were successful not so much because of specific techniques they developed, nor even because of an overall program. The program is based on an underlying philosophy, made up of several fundamental principles. The preceding chapters on team leadership share this philosophy and these principles. They, as we, believe that people at all levels of society, when trusted enough to be empowered, will take ownership for solving problems with a great deal of insight and enthusiasm. This trust requires leaders who can see strengths where others see weaknesses. It is based on the belief that treating people with dignity brings out the best in them. Leaders who want to bring about these results need a great deal of vision, patience, and commitment. But, they will be richly rewarded.

Chapter Application Exercises
A. Personal Inventory
The following questions are designed to help you determine whether you are headed for burnout. There is no particular number of questions that would indicate that is the direction you are heading because some people are much more resilient than others. Simply reflect on these questions to determine what aspects of your life (or of your work) you may wish to change.
1. Do you get tired easily?
2. Do you frequently feel like you are working harder and harder, but getting less done?
3. Are you spending less time with people that are important to you?
4. Do you often feel tired of trying?
5. Do you frequently feel that your efforts are unnoticed, or that people don't care?
6. Do you get sick frequently?
7. Do you have trouble feeling good around other people?
8. Do you enjoy your work most of the time?
9. Do you find yourself avoiding social occasions more than you used to?
10. Do you have trouble relaxing?
11. Do you feel that you don't care as much as you used to about the success or failure of people in your program?
12. Do you sometimes feel trapped in your job?
13. Do you still have hobbies and outside activities that you can "lose yourself" in?
14. Do you seem to lose your temper more than you used to?
15. Do you have people that you can confide in and do you listen as much as you talk?
B. Group Exercise
As a team, discuss the following questions to evaluate the training and staff development you have had during the past year:

1. How much has it changed your behavior?
2. Has there been follow-up to make sure that people are using the new techniques, principles or action?
3. Do you follow up from previous training when you move on to the next topic?
4. Is your training focused on your vision of what you want to be as a group? Have you identified what training will be needed to get you there?
5. Do you use pre-assessment to see what training is needed?
6. Which individuals in your organization could serve as models of past training topics? Are they being used for this purpose?
7. Do you make it safe for people to try out new skills? Do you expect change and support it in each other?

Now, discuss how you may want to change the way you do training.

Chapter Notes

---

1 Based on statement by M.Russell Ballard, Duncan and Pinegar, *Leadership for Saints*, 120.

2 Daniel Goleman, *Working with Emotional Intelligence*.

3 Goleman, *Working with Emotional Intelligence*, 249.

4 Edward T. Joyner, "No More 'Drive-By Staff Development," in Peter Senge (ed) *Schools that Learn*, 385-395.

5 From anonymous interview with Early Head Start Director, May, 2001.

6 Studs Terkel, *Working*.

7 Christina Maslach and Michael P. Leiter, *The Truth About Burnout* (New York: Josey-Bass, 1997).

8 Duncan and Pinegar, 299.

9 Adapted from Katharine Briar-Larson. "The Rainmakers", in Peter Senge (Ed.), *Schools That Learn* (New York: Currency, 2000), 529-538.

Chapter 8.
"Getting the Boss on Board."
Managing Relationships with Your Boss

Chapter Summary

Many early childhood program leaders have success in getting their staff to apply the principles of team leadership only to find their boss less willing to do so. Books about "Managing Your Boss" suggest strategies that are manipulative, or possibly unethical. This chapter describes ways to work with even the most difficult bosses, applying many of the same principles presented in the preceding chapters.

> Comedian Bill Cosby tells a story about his high-school football days. His team had a tough game and was behind when it went to the locker room at halftime. The coach really lit into them. Pretty soon, he had them screaming for blood. They were going to <u>kill</u> the other team. Then, at the climactic moment, he yelled for them to get out on the field and do it! They jumped up as one and ran screaming to the door-only to find it was locked from the other side!

Team Management Without the Full Support of Your Boss

Getting your staff excited and working as a team can be like this experience if someone in upper administration blocks your efforts. Some bosses fight team management because they think workers need to be controlled, not consulted. Others resist because they think a boss is supposed to make all the decisions. Bosses from some cultural backgrounds believe that letting subordinates participate in decision-making is an admission of their own ignorance and uncertainty. Still other bosses would like to try team leadership, but feel they can't risk it because they are under pressure to get immediate results.

If you have worked many years in organizations, you are almost sure to have had at least one "bad boss." Some of these bosses may resist or undermine team leadership. Others may abuse the authority of their positions. In a few rare instances, even people who are borderline mental cases make it into leadership positions. Regardless of how they get there, a bad boss can stifle initiative, create havoc, and turn an organization into chaos. Knowing how to deal with such situations is very important.

In most cases, however, the problem with a "bad boss" can be more accurately seen as the result of a poorly-handled relationship. If this is true in your case, you can improve the relationship by changing the way you interact with your boss. In this chapter, we will explore some proven ways to handle these relationships.

Basic Principles of Dealing With a Difficult Boss

A 1992 study commissioned by an insurance company asked 28,000 workers to name the principle causes of work stress.[1] Most workers cited a bad relationship with the boss as the main cause. In addition, a poor relationship with one's boss was associated with low morale, high absenteeism, and even physical problems (like stomach ailments). In fact, the stress from a poor relationship with their boss was even worse for some workers than was stress caused by some of life's worst traumas (including death of a spouse or other close relatives).

Similarly, in a study of over 1,000 college students, the first-ranked job fear was "that I will find myself working under superiors who I will not be able to respect or follow with real commitment.[2] Women generally report poorer relationships with their bosses than men do, even when the boss is a female.[3] Studies of workplace "bullying" suggest that this may be more the result of the cultural perception that women are less likely than men to stand up to bullying[4] than to any inability of women to handle relationships with their boss.

Whenever most of us have a problem with the boss, it is tempting to claim we have a bad boss. Closer examination often shows that the perception of a bad boss is better explained as the result of a bad situation, as the following episode reported by an ECI program director suggests.

> A year ago, my staff and I went through a wonderful week-long training on family-centered interdisciplinary teaming. It encouraged us to help parents set priorities for their child and family. It prompted us to look at relationships with parents as partnerships rather than teacher-pupil situations. It was inspired training that started the whole team in a new worthwhile direction. After the training, we spent many hours as a team, problem-solving and offering support to each other. It was an incredibly creative time [when] strong relationships were built throughout the program and with the parents.
>
> Then, as they say, "the wheels fell off." The State Legislature

began asking about accountability, and "best value" became a new buzzword. All of a sudden we had to turn in monthly hours of direct service, travel, evaluations, and case management. We were told to meet with any staff member who was not meeting state averages. The State implemented a database that allowed them to monitor any employee anywhere in the state, showing their case load, hours of services, Medicaid dollars brought in, etc. They rewarded individuals for high percentages of successfully-delivered services. To get the high percentages, our staff began "hounding" families to keep appointments, even when it was inconvenient for them. A "Big Brother" mentality began and trust dissolved.

Everything we had accomplished changed! Staff became discouraged, paranoid, and even pushy. Instead of loving my job and feeling passionate about our role to help families, I dreaded going to work. Now, my job involved auditing charts, logs and reimbursement figures and pressuring staff members to reach their quotas. We stopped meeting regularly as a team because the paperwork became overwhelming. I received more parent complaints than ever before. Instead of the compassionate, supportive individuals we once were, we had become robots in our obsession to meet quotas.

This incident illustrates the frustration that team leaders can run into when higher administration blocks team leadership. It also shows how problems that get blamed on a boss or team leader may, in fact, be the result of a bad situation. The director of this program was pressured into abandoning team leadership and felt compelled to start pushing her staff to meet quotas. They increasingly saw her as pushy and distant. Likewise, the parents began to believe that she and her staff did not care about them or their personal situations. In short, a bad situation created the mistaken impression that a very caring and highly capable person was a "bad boss." Let's examine some principles that will help you deal with any problems with your boss.

A. Determine Whether It's Situational and Not A Personal Flaw.

This was a point we emphasized in Chapter One. Bad situations can cause people to do things which end up looking like personality defects. Earlier, we presented the case of a hospital receiving clerk who was blamed for being crotchety and rude. A closer look revealed that too many people were able to give him orders. A similar outcome was found in restaurants that had frequent conflict between waitresses and cooks. In each case, the organizational situation, rather than anyone's personality, was the underlying cause of the problems.

Most of us have an easier time accepting "the power of the situation" as an explanation of problems with co-workers than we do when the boss is involved. After all, if bosses have more power, they should be able to control work situations. Though bosses do tend to have more authority than those below them, they also have bosses (and government officials) who impose difficult situations on them. Sometimes, the power of such situations is hidden. As a result, many child care professionals and parents in early childhood organizations tend to blame the director, rather than bad situations, for their problems and frustrations.

This is not to say that there are not bad bosses. The world has many people who abuse power, bully subordinates, or otherwise create havoc in the workplace. Power can have a corrupting influence on some individuals. Indeed, when people get together to tell organizational war stories, it's hard to find any "veteran" that has not had at least one experience with a truly bad boss.

In reality, this reinforces our point about the power of the situation. Situations not only cause problems to be misinterpreted as personality defects; they can also create, or even magnify, personal defects. The situation of absolute power, for example, has a well-known tendency (some would say certainty) to corrupt absolutely. Even ordinary people can be affected by powerful situations. Milgram's experiment, described in Chapter Three, showed that two-thirds of ordinary people put in a situation of "teacher" went to the extreme of administering "shocks" that could be considered as torture. But these people were not silent sadists. They were ordinary people in a difficult situation. Before we consider how to deal with a "bad boss," let's look at how we might improve relationships by understanding (and adjusting to) bad situations.

One way to improve the relationship with your boss might be to better understand the structural pressures she faces. Though you might not be able to change her situation, it might make you more understanding. In addition, your team might be able to give her much appreciated support, which can only help the relationship.

It is easy when confronted with a "petty tyrant" to assume that his or her behavior is the result of "warped" personality. Rosbeth Kanter, a sociologist, found that power given to the boss position, more than the personality of the boss, is the best predictor of how people in these positions will behave as bosses. Bosses, male or female, whose position gives them little authority to make important decisions often become punitive, petty tyrants. Blocked from exercising power in the wider hierarchy, they substitute the satisfaction of lording it over subordinates. Unable to move ahead, they hold everyone back. In contrast, bosses in positions with real authority tend to be more flexible about rules, to share information with employees, and to try to help able ones move on to better jobs.[5]

If your boss is like the "petty tyrant" just described, consider the possibility that she is kept on a pretty short leash by higher-ups in your organization. For example, if her boss has a tendency to micro-manage it will create a difficult situation for her, and you and your team are likely to suffer the consequences. If you suspect that such is the case, you and your team can be more understanding and look for ways to be supportive. Part of the reason tightly-controlled bosses do not get much support from below, however, is because the people they work with think they have a personality problem. If you can get past that, your support will confer "authority from below," or the same team support that you find empowering.

Another structural factor that may foster unpleasant behavior from a boss is the degree of creativity and freedom her position provides. The story of the ECI director a few pages back is a good illustration of this. When she and her team were free to explore better ways to help the parents and children, the work was exciting and stimulating. When her job was redefined to make her someone who monitors performance statistics, ("We had become robots in our obsession to meet quotas") she dreaded going to work. It is likely that both her staff and the parents began to see this change as a personality issue.

Studies by Melvin Kohn and Carmi Schooler show these effects on personality. Jobs that encourage self-direction or that allow someone to work at their own pace and be more intellectually active, produce flexible, open, and less authoritarian attitudes. Constricted, boring, routine jobs that give people no room to spread their wings tend to dampen self-esteem and make people in these positions more rigid and intolerant. Frequently, people whose job allows them more room for self-direction voluntarily put in longer hours with minimal complaints.[6]

While the studies cited do not reveal how one can deal with bosses in these situations, they do help us understand that the job situation itself, as well as a superior's personality, can make life difficult for those who work with them. We would hope that such understanding would help you and your team members have a bit more patience as you explore ways to help a boss who has been difficult to work with.

Though it may be comforting to learn that difficult bosses often get that way because of job pressures, we still have to work with them. The greatest assistance we can offer to those in such situations is to present some basic principles and practices that have proven effective in dealing with a difficult boss.

B. Avoid Manipulative Methods, Like "Managing Your Boss"

First, we should clarify what we mean by a "difficult boss" and show how one differs from a truly "bad boss." There are many books and even some web sites that focus on bad bosses. Basic to all of their discussions is the idea that bad bosses are those who have "stepped over the line" in the use of authority. We can illustrate this by referring to the types of power shown in Figure 8.1, "Types of Power."

The main difference between you as a "subordinate" and your boss is the authority delegated to the position occupied by your boss. Authority, the third type of power shown in the figure, can be defined as the legitimate right to use (or threaten to use) force, either in the form of withholding rewards or administering punishment. Most bosses seldom have to use force, but the right to do so gives them authority. Likewise, a boss can try to persuade you by using influence. However, when his or her efforts to do so become illegitimate, he or she has slipped "over the line" into manipulation.

Most problems of bad or difficult bosses

Figure 8.1

Types of Power

	Legitimate Uses Of Power	Illegitimate Uses Of Power
Accomplished by Persuasion	Influence	Manipulation
Accomplished by Force (or the Threat of Force)	Authority	Coercion

revolve around their use of force and influence. The bully is a boss who uses coercion to push people around, using force in illegitimate ways. A prime example is the superior who tries to use his position to get intimacy from female subordinates. The "wimp" is afraid to use influence or authority when these are needed. On the other hand, the "manipulator" is one who uses deceit and dishonesty to get people to go along. A boss who repeatedly asks people to do extra work, saying it's "for the children," but who in reality cares little about the children, would be a manipulator.

Team leadership is about using influence to accomplish organizational purposes. A good team leader seldom has to use authority to force people to go along. Bureaucratic bosses, in contrast, rely heavily on authority. Often, the result they get is workers who do only as much as they are "forced" to do.

Difficult bosses occasionally resort to bullying or manipulation. Really bad bosses **are** bullies, wimps, and manipulators. People who work with them feel abused and demeaned. Sometimes, people higher up in the hierarchy tolerate or even support bullies because they seem able to force people to get work done. This might have worked several decades ago, but today the price of bullying is high turnover, low morale, and workers who do only as much as they have to. Organizations that tolerate bullying are not pleasant places to work.

Some management consultants approach the problem of bullies and manipulators by suggesting techniques that can also be manipulative. Often, they suggest tricking the boss into doing something by using questionable tactics. Some of the most blatant suggestions include flattering your boss before asking for something or deliberately putting something bad into a proposal so your boss can feel useful when he insists you take it out. Another manipulative suggestion is to "go around" your boss by becoming friendly with his or her boss.

Mark Maletz, a prominent consultant, questions the core of the "How to Manage Your Boss" lore. He says that this gives you the notion:

> that somehow you are smarter and more enlightened, informed and capable than your boss. The problem with this fable is the realization that you yourself did not stumble over your brilliant insight or ingenious project in one glorious moment. Undoubtedly, you arrived at your idea over time. It was a process. When your boss doesn't understand your ideas immediately, don't label him or her an ignorant bureaucrat. That attitude will back your boss against a wall and make it difficult for you to get your idea across. Instead, recognize that your boss has to go through a similar journey of understanding that you traveled to "get there." [7]

Stephen Covey, author and leadership consultant also advises against using influence in illegitimate ways.

> Don't let yourself become a victim of your boss's weaknesses. And stop looking for evidence to justify your feelings about your terrible boss: how he's the source of your career block...If you fall into these habits, you'll become afflicted with the cancers of the workplace: complaining, criticizing, comparing and competing. Instead, focus on your own circle of influence—all those things over which you have control. First, make sure your own job is in order. Credibility is something you can earn gradually by becoming one of the best performers in the organization. Others will begin to have more faith and confidence in you because they respect you, and know you won't be talking about them behind their backs. Finally, understand where your boss is coming from. Nothing is more validating and affirming than feeling understood. The moment the person begins feeling understood by you, that person becomes much more open to influence and change. Learn and practice the art of personal leadership and see how it inspires those around you-including your boss."[8]

C. Use the <u>Principles</u> of Team Leadership.

Covey's statement emphasizes several of the principles of team leadership. We do not need to be manipulative if we apply the principles of team leadership presented with the boss as well as with each other. Team leadership is about using sound principles to internally motivate people. With the possible exception of really bad bosses (which we'll discuss later in the chapter), the principles of team leadership will work as well with your boss as they do with your team. Specifically, let's examine how the principles of high expectations, win-win relationships, creating a sense of ownership, and commitment to a cause can help you "manage" this relationship, even with difficult bosses.

1. High Expectations. The statement by Covey states, *"Nothing* *is more validating and affirming than feeling understood. The moment the person begins feeling understood by you, that person becomes much more open to influence and change."* People feel understood when we acknowledge the difficulties they face and when we see them more in terms of their strengths than their weaknesses. This is why it is so important to understand the structural pressures a boss faces. It makes us more willing to understand that their behavior may be caused by more than a personality flaw.

Understanding someone also requires that we avoid what Covey referred to above as the cancers of "complaining and criticizing." When people sit around and criticize their boss (or a co-worker), they lower their expectations of that person. We emphasized in earlier chapters the power of positive expectations. We all perform better when someone expects great things of us because they see strengths that we might not even see ourselves. Remember, "What you see is what you'll get."

If you frequently criticize your boss, you will actually be contributing to the problems you are complaining about. Criticizing makes it virtually impossible to have high expectations. The best support you can give a boss is to actually *see* strengths. When you do (and this is what you share with your co-workers), you won't need to utter a single word of flattery to have a positive impact on his or her behavior.

2. Win-Win Relationships. Because bosses have authority, they are in a position to control rewards or administer punishment. Often, that fact creates an "us-versus-them" mentality which can get highly competitive. Perhaps this is what Covey means by the other two cancers he mentions "comparing and competing." In highly competitive situations, we give as little as we can, hoping to get as much as possible in return. Competitive work situations are characterized by workers who do as little as they can get away with, while all the while pressuring to get greater and greater rewards. This mentality frequently causes organizations afflicted with it to self-destruct with constant labor strikes and management retaliation.

The opposite, of course, is a win-win relationship in which each party recognizes the needs of the other and looks for ways to get the most benefits for both sides. Cooperative relationships like this can only exist where there is considerable trust. If either party does not trust the other, they will fall back on the win-lose mentality. We need to approach all interactions with our boss with the aim of doing as much to meet his or her needs as we hope they will do for ours.

In early childhood organizations, the win-lose mentality affects children and families the most. This is reflected in an African proverb that states, "When elephants fight, it is the grass that suffers." If you become locked in a win-lose battle with your boss, the children and families will inevitably suffer.

3. Creating a Sense of Ownership. In many organizations, bosses are the ones who feel ownership for the well-being of the organization and for solving problems. Team leadership often involves getting people at lower levels to feel ownership. This is done, as we mentioned in previous chapters, by gradually empowering workers to solve problems and achieve goals without having to ask the boss's permission on everything.

For many bosses, the hardest part of sharing ownership is sharing authority. Some do not trust workers because they continue to believe that subordinates are competitors (the win-lose mentality). Others feel that they will lose authority if they empower workers (actually, they will, so you must help them see that influence works better than *authority* in child care programs).

Be careful, though. The creation of teams is not meant to take ownership away from a boss. It is more about *sharing* ownership than *transferring* it. The best way to share ownership with your boss is to do everything possible to include him or her as part of the team. Some bosses will resist this because they have been taught that leadership means being above and distant from those they lead.

If bosses tend to be aloof, involve them as much as possible in team activities. Invite them to occasionally get down on the floor with the children and to make occasional visits to the families. Encourage them to participate in team celebrations and to join with you in having fun together.

4. Commitment to a Cause. If you frequently find yourself and your boss on different sides of things, the best solution is to get together on the same side—that of the children. Sharing a common cause, especially when we feel deeply about it, brings us closer as does finding ways to cooperate to accomplish our mission as part of a larger cause.

Perhaps the best way to do this is to put the boss in a leadership role related to this cause as often as possible. For example, you might ask him or her to take some time with your staff to help all of you revisit the reasons you are involved in early childhood education. It would be wonderful if the boss could work as a colleague when you define your mission or chart a vision. This might best be accomplished by using a moderator during such exercises. A moderator temporarily gives authority to an outsider, thus making your boss one of the group, with no more authority during the exercise than others in the group.

The more you apply the principles of team leadership, the more successful you will become in improving the relationship with your boss. When this individual shares your excitement for team leadership, you will have a very fruitful relationship. If not, then work with patience to get him or her to understand at the same level you do. Remember the statement quoted earlier from Maletz: "You arrived at your idea over time. It was a process. When your boss doesn't understand your ideas immediately, don't label him or her an ignorant bureaucrat... Instead, recognize that your boss has to go through a similar journey of understanding that you traveled to 'get there.'

D. Use the *Skills* of Team Leadership.

The skills we have presented in earlier chapters also work well in dealing with your boss. Regardless of whether he or she is "difficult," or wonderful, these skills are essential to a productive relationship. The most useful will probably be effective communications and conflict resolution, though these also involve skill of summarizing and establishing clear ground rules. Let's briefly review the skills just mentioned with reference to their application to the relationship with your boss.

1. Effective Communication. There is hardly a book on bosses that does not stress the importance of good communications. Bosses can get especially upset if they feel uninformed. Most superiors are willing to give you room to work if you keep them informed. They especially want to know about things that have the potential to get them in trouble with their own superiors, so do not allow them to get "blindsided." If you see a problem coming, give your boss a "heads-up," then indicate what you are doing to deal with the situation.

Whenever you receive instructions from your boss, check understanding to make sure you have correctly grasped what he or she is asking of you. During a meeting, this is done by indicating that you want to be sure you have understood correctly and then summarizing what your boss has just said. Following the close of your meeting, write this down. Many individuals find e-mail especially useful for this purpose. It's informal enough that it does not appear you are overdoing the "written record," but still gives you a physical reminder of your agreement. This may be especially important if there has been a misunderstanding, or even a "blow-up," with your boss. As soon as you collect your thoughts and your wit, write a summary of what you understood was said and what was asked of you. Be especially careful to keep this document focused on the essence of what was discussed.

There is nothing wrong with wanting to make sure you do not misunderstand. Merely saying you are doing so should not put your boss on the defensive. You are simply trying to ensure that you understood correctly, without any criticism of how clearly he or she might have communicated. Finally, if there has been serious disagreement, you will have the protection of a written record of what you both said or agreed to.

2. Conflict Resolution. Even in the best relationships with a boss, there will likely be occasional conflict. If discussions of your differences do not get "out of bounds," they can usually produce many positive effects, such as allowing people to feel strongly about something and helping them clarify issues. More important than having a peaceful relationship with your boss is the need for that relationship to be effective. While some people never fight, they may also never resolve basic underlying issues. Conflict can bring things out in the open where they can be resolved. For this reason, it is more important to resolve conflict with your boss than it is to be able to avoid it.

If conflict arises, remember that anger and deep-seated emotions should be kept in check. Should they start getting out of control, you have several options. First, you may suggest that each of you state what he or she thinks the other is saying, with you offering to go first. If necessary, you may then request time to consider what that person is saying, thus indicating that you will get back to him or her after you have had some time to think about it. If possible, agree on when that time will be.

Finally, if things start getting personal, with some "hitting below the belt" occurring, you may call a "time out" to see if you can agree on some basic ground rules. You do not have to endure abusive language, name calling, or bullying. Encounters that have gotten to that point should shift focus to treating each other with civility. You can and should insist on being treated with respect (more about this later in the chapter).

Once you get the discussion back on track, try to find out what your boss really needs. Intense feelings usually lead to people taking a position. Searching for a win-win solution requires that you actively try to find a way to meet the needs of your boss, even as you attempt to meet your own needs. Make sure that you also state what you need, as opposed to just drawing a line in the sand (taking a position). Again, it's often good to give yourself some time to find ways to craft win-win solutions. If it does not violate confidentiality, you may even involve your team in developing such a solution. Just be careful that you do not end up making this a session on airing complaints against your boss.

Most Difficult Cases--Self-Defense Tactics Against a Really Bad Boss

John is one of the most outstanding individuals I have ever worked with. When he was a consultant for me, I knew that he would always deliver the highest quality work. John would always add a touch of class and quality to any project. He would take an important task, involve others, give good feedback and help everyone contribute to the result.

I had not seen John for 15 years until I ran into him as I was giving a talk. He invited me into his work area and was telling me about a very interesting project he was involved with. While I was talking to him, his boss came by. The boss asked John in an angry voice where a proposal was. John's face changed. A worried look appeared on his face, and he began scrambling to meet the demands of his boss. I had never seen John so uncomfortable.

It took him several minutes to locate the proposal, and the boss became increasingly impatient. When John finally found the proposal, the boss stormed off visibly angry about the response time. I was appalled by this interaction between John and his boss. He later told me that this interaction was typical-that this was the way he treated everyone. It was terribly sad to see what this type of treatment was doing to a wonderful person.[9]

John's boss was a bully. As his case illustrates, bullies cause enormous harm to individuals and to their workplace. Nothing goes more against the principles of team leadership than bullying. Bullying is about control. It is oriented toward one person winning at the expense of another's humiliation or loss. If you tolerate bullying in your workplace, everyone will suffer.

Some people bully others because they are insecure sociopaths. They enjoy feeling in control, and they enjoy the suffering they cause their victims. The best thing you can do if one of these gets you in his or her sights is to get out of the way. If your organization tolerates or encourages such behavior, your talents will be much better used elsewhere. It is very unlikely you can change a bully who is a sociopath. Such people leave a trail of victims in their path of destruction. Don't be one of these victims.

Other bullies think it is part of a game. They see management as intense competition in which the "fittest" (or most aggressive) rise to the top by conquering all competitors. For example, one lawyer at a San Francisco firm claims, "*bullying has its benefits. This country was built by mean, aggressive SOBs. Would Microsoft have made so many millionaires if Bill Gates had not been so aggressive?....Some people may need a little appropriate bullying in order to do a good job.*"[10]

The mentality behind this form of bullying, as the quote illustrates, is that people must be motivated from without. Again, this flies in the face of team leadership. It violates the principles of ownership, exploits the idea of a great cause as a manipulative trick, and conceives teamwork as doing what you are told (by the head bully). This form of thinking can be very destructive in early childhood agencies.

Fortunately, this line of reasoning is less common in early childhood education than it is in the world of business or educational administration. Still, some workplaces do have a problem with bullies. The more common forms of bullying, as distinguished from occasional incivility or rudeness, include the following: exaggerated blaming of the intended "victim" for errors; making unreasonable job demands; harping criticism of ability; threatening job loss; insults and put-downs; discounting or denying accomplishments; yelling and screaming, and stealing credit for accomplishments of the intended victim.

How can you respond to a boss who bullies you? One study[11] of bullying around the world asked people who had been bullied at work what they would have done differently. The top response was that they should have *stood up to the bully*, especially when it started. In addition, they felt they should have *gotten help to stop the bullying*. Victims often said it would have been wise to *keep a detailed journal* of the incidents in order to establish the **pattern** of bullying. Finally, they felt they should have *recognized that the bully was really a coward* who picks on people because he or she perceives them to be weak.

Studies such as these indicate that you can stop a bully from making you a victim. Many of the steps to stopping it are the same as those used to stop spousal abuse. First, don't let the bully convince you that you are the problem. Victims often detect a grain of truth in an attack, eventually coming to believe that their inadequacies are causing the bully to get angry.

You can stop this by not letting someone speak to you in a way that is demeaning, or intended to hurt. All of us make errors and have weaknesses. Someone giving constructive criticism, or even chastising us for an error brings up the failing without a personal attack intended to hurt. Often, you can decide whether it's bullying or constructive criticism more by the tone than by the content. When you hear such an attack coming, do not become defensive about the supposed weakness. Raise your objection to the attack itself. You might say something like, "Stop! I do not appreciate being talked to like that." You might express your willingness to discuss your performance, but be firm as you indicate that you will do it only if and when it does not sound like a personal attack. If the bully is willing to proceed in that way, briefly summarize his or her criticisms to make sure you understand. This allows you to center the discussion on behavior, rather than endure a personal attack.

Stanley Bing, in his book *Crazy Bosses*, gives an example of this type of response.

> My first boss was a woman with a foul temper who tormented anyone who would let her. When she started to yell and tear paper, I would simply say, "Excuse me, April, I think I have a call on hold." And I would stroll out of her office. Later, I would poke my head in on some pretext and re-establish relations. After a while, she learned that it wasn't much fun to bully me.[12]

Suzette Elgin, in her book *The Gentle Art of Verbal Self Defense at Work*,[13] proposes that bullies demonstrate a pattern in their attacks that can be easily recognized. Essentially, it involves a "hook" or "bait" by which they attempt to draw you into a conflict. If you cave in, or if you respond defensively, they win. A victory to the bully is to beat you down or draw you into conflict. With either of these responses, you lose.

The appropriate response is, first of all, not to cave in. Do not think that by agreeing with an attack, the bully will feel sorry and let up. You will be setting yourself up for more attacks in the future.

Second, do not take the bait. Respond instead to the supposed error upon which the bait is based. This allegation is often unstated. The bully may imply it without coming right out and stating it. The bait is a personal attack on you. The supposed error is the basis, again either stated or implied, upon which the attack is based. If someone states, for example, "You can't do anything right," the bait is the implied meaning that you are worthless. It is based on some supposed error--that you have done something wrong. Again, ignore the bait and respond to the supposed error. Following our example, you might say something like, "I recognize that you are not satisfied with how I handled ___. Could you please let me know how I might have handled it differently?"

Let's discuss one more example to make this pattern clear.

He leaned back comfortably in his swivel chair behind the elegant desk, placed both hands behind his head in an attitude of pure superiority and said condescendingly (while rolling his eyes and shaking his head), "No one really reads your newsletters. Mostly, I find them in the trash around here."

You are stunned, confused, and hurt. All your life you have been complimented on your writing ability, and you know lots of folks who love your newsletters. In fact, you feel this is something you enjoy and do well. Why would a supervisor not see the gift you are giving to his organization with your talents?

The abuse in this account is somewhat subtle, but enough to make the target begin to doubt her abilities. The abusive nature of the comment is evident, not only in its implications, but in the tone and body language by which it was given. The bait is "You are a lousy writer," so that should be ignored.

Instead, she should respond to the supposed error--that newsletters in the trash indicate that she did a poor job of writing. She could ask, for example, "When did you first notice that the newsletters were not being read (or that they are being discarded)?" Or, she could go to a more impersonal mode and say something like, "It's interesting that some people believe that a newsletter in the trashcan has not been read." Perhaps better still an even more direct approach would be to ask, "What specific problems do you have with my newsletters?"

Of course, not all of us can think quickly on our feet in light of a provocative attack. Don't allow your natural hesitation to formulate a clever rejoinder keep you from responding. You will get better with practice. If nothing else, work on your own thinking, and start by refusing to be (or even see yourself as) a victim. You are not powerless, and you can set limits that will be honored. Approximately 75 percent of people do not tolerate being bullied. You can be one of them.

There are several ways to keep from becoming a victim. You need to use anger only when it is a positive emotion and get rid of it when it is not. It is positive only when it helps with "fight or flight" response. In such cases, anger may be a wonderful short-term way of getting you out of trouble. But there are few situations in early childhood programs when acting out anger is the best response. Anger only helps when acting on it helps resolve the problem.

Once the situation has passed, the long-term effects of holding (and expressing) anger are only negative. Your nervous system cannot tell whether the danger you are seeing is occurring now or ten years ago, so you keep turning on chemicals in the body that damage your health and alter your ability to think clearly. Anger, held and nourished for extended periods of time, traps you in a vicious circle of hurt and physical discomfort.

Many of us learned early in life to suppress our anger out of the fear that it might cause us to do something we would later regret. But anger can be brief and well-channeled. The simple statement, "I will not be treated like that," is a positive and well-controlled use of anger.

Perhaps the biggest obstacle to standing up to a bully is fear. We believe that we might lose our job. We are afraid to "make waves." If we continue to let fear keep us from acting, we will find ourselves believing what the bully says about us. We will also let it keep us from doing things that are really needed by the children and families in our care.

This is illustrated by the investigation of an Air Florida crash into the Potomac River in 1982. The investigators attributed the crash to "pilot error." More accurately, however, it should have been attributed to "relationship failure." The pilot misread his data, thinking he had enough thrust for takeoff. His co-pilot knew of the error, but was reluctant to challenge the tradition and authority of the pilot. Because he was afraid to question the pilot's judgment, all but five people were killed in the accident.[14]

Getting along with your boss is important. It makes for a nice work situation. But getting along well is not the main thing toward which to strive. Even more important is learning to be effective together. Sometimes, that may require you to stand up for yourself and for the program. That is what you were hired for and that is what the children and families need from us.

If fear stops you from taking a stand, consider the example of the student civil rights workers who stood up to the violence of segregation. Many were extremely afraid. They worked together, however, to overcome the fear. They went through role playing. They gave each other positive support. They went to jail together and found that they really could handle all the things they had feared. Together, they became some of the most powerful agents for change in the history of the United States.

If you have had many experiences with bullies in your life, your greatest problem today is probably that of having to overcome the hurt. Many otherwise bright and capable people can be restricted for life by the grudges and hurt they feel. Grudges are especially bad because they make you see yourself as a victim. You are only a victim if you feel unable to control what happens to you.

Holding in hurt as grudges can become an obsession. It keeps you from focusing on your larger goals-the things that matter most in your life and in your work. Fred Luskin in his book, *Forgive for Good: A Proven Prescription for Health and Happiness*[15] describes the health and mental benefits of getting rid of grudges. Learning to forgive, he says, does <u>not</u> mean you condone hurtful behavior. Neither does it mean that you let someone abuse you. Letting go of grudges, or forgiving, is more for your benefit than it is for the person who hurt you. It allows you to take control of your life and your emotions.

On the basis of extensive research, Luskin says that you will know if you are obsessing over a hurt if you realize that you are thinking about it too much, if you find yourself telling your grievance story over and over, or if you discover a personal inability to appreciate the beautiful and wonderful things in your life. Let's briefly examine each of these.

You are thinking about it too much, or obsessing, if you start losing sleep over what happened. Also, if time away from work is dominated by thoughts of the hurt, it is on your mind too much. People who handle stress the best know how to leave a hurt aside until they can deal effectively with it. They are able to throw themselves into some activity and focus entirely on it. Luskin advises us to ask how much space in our mind we are "renting out" to the bully. Don't let bullies have control of your mind.

Next, look to see if you are telling your grievance story over and over. A grievance is something that happened that we did not want to happen (or that we did not handle appropriately). A grievance is a hurt, plus outrage and obsession. More important than the constant retelling, however, is that people who obsess about a hurt tell the story in a way that they are no longer the central character. It is the bully, or the evil perpetrator, who has ruined their life.

Finally, you are obsessing if you let a grudge make you tune out the larger things in your life. It makes you focus on what went wrong, rather than what went right. It also makes you feel a "victim," or someone powerless against opposition. This actually increases the ability of a bully to torment you. In addition, it keeps you constantly stressed out, emotionally upset, drained, and sick. Over time, the grudge will begin to ruin your relationships with people who matter most because they will eventually get tired of hearing your grievances. It will also keep you from seeing yourself as the part of a community that your team and your family need you to be.

In short, holding on to hurt makes a bad situation worse. You can keep a hurt from becoming a grievance or a grudge if you force yourself to not take it too personally, if you quit blaming the offender for how you feel, and if you don't let the hurt become a grievance story.

So how can you turn loose of hurt? Start by realizing that forgiving someone does not mean you accept their harmful behavior. Rather, it simply means turning loose of the idea that they owe you a debt. Forgiving cancels a perceived debt, it does not condone wrong behavior. Next try to see the non-personal aspects of the injury. Did the bully single you out, or were you simply a convenient target when the mood struck. Realize that being hurt is a very common experience. You can see that others have experienced similar hurt and not let it ruin their lives. This does not mean pretending there was no personal hurt-only that you keep it in perspective by recognizing the non-personal aspects of the experience.

Next, stop blaming. Examine other possible reasons why you were hurt. Even if you decide the bully alone is responsible for the pain inflicted, you can hold that person accountable for their actions without blaming them. Remember, when we blame bullies, we give them power over how we feel.

Getting Out of the Box

Our tendency to blame others for wrongs, real or imagined, creates another set of problems for us. This is outlined by the Arbinger Institute, an organization for individuals and organizations seeking to end self-destructive behavior resulting from serious emotional scars. In their excellent book, *Leadership and Self-Deception: Getting out of the Box,*[16] they point out how some natural human tendencies put us in "a box." The "box" is our inability to see things truthfully and live up to principles we really believe in.

Bullies, however, do not put us in the box. We get ourselves there when we engage in self-betrayal. A self-betrayal results from not doing something we know we should, or doing something to someone when we know we shouldn't. Self-betrayal is an act contrary to what we feel is right.

This point of view rests on the idea that all of us have a difficult time living with inconsistency in ourselves (sometimes referred to as "Cognitive Dissonance" Theory). When we know we have violated some basic standards of right and wrong, we can either change our behavior (less common), or try to justify having behaved this way (most common). We accomplish this self-justification in at least two ways: First, we mentally exaggerate how bad the other person is (for example, seeing them as mean, lazy, inconsiderate, unappreciative, insensitive, or evil). This helps convince us that they really deserve bad treatment.

The second way we justify treating someone badly is to exaggerate our good characteristics (for example, thinking we are sensitive, fair, hardworking, or all- suffering). By this second exaggeration, we tend to see ourselves as a victim of the bad person. This second exaggeration also includes blowing out of proportion the importance of the work we do in order to justify our behavior. For example, if we have so much to do and we are so important, then some "ruffling of feathers" cannot be avoided.

Both of these exaggerations are distortions of reality, but they help us justify in our own minds the betrayal of our moral compass. We need these distortions to prevent "dissonance," or feeling that we have betrayed our principles. But, we have to convince ourselves that these distortions are accurate in order to feel good about ourselves. This betrayal of principles, along with our distortions of reality, put us in "the box."

Another part of being in the box is our tendency to treat other people as objects. This also makes it easier to violate principles without feeling guilty. The authors use the example of a man in an airplane with open seating. He doesn't want to be crowded, but he also knows he should take into consideration other people's need to find a seat. If he sees other people as objects, however, he can put his briefcase on one seat and spread out his newspaper to try to keep anyone from sitting next to him because others are not real people to him.

This self-betrayal and our attempts to justify it through self-deception put us, so to speak, "in the box." Amazingly, however, most people who are in the box cannot see themselves as part of the problem. Ask yourself, for example, how many people who cause serious problems really believe that they cause these dilemmas. Most problem- causers, we think you'll agree, are in denial. This is why they are in the box.

Now, let's pose the hard question. If most people who cause problems are in denial (and in the box), is it possible that each of us may be in the same situation? Could we be in the box in relation to problems we are having with our boss? Indeed, when one person is in the box, his or her behavior often provokes others to be there also. Then, each is so busy blaming the other that they cannot see that they are contributing to the problem.

It is important to understand that we tend to blame others because we want to justify ourselves, not because we want to help them. Blaming is also not about trying to bring out the truth. The most common result of blaming is to make someone become defensive, pushing them into their own box. Then, they blame us for unfairly blaming them. As a result, we start provoking each other to do the very things we find offensive. This mutual "invitation" to do the wrong thing, and then blame each other for it, is called collusion.

The authors provide the following example to show the effects of mutual blaming.

A mother is having problems with her 18-year-old son. He frequently stays out late, not telling her where he is going. Because she's in the box in relation to him, she starts mentally blaming him for being irresponsible, disrespectful, and troublesome. She criticizes his behavior when they talk. Then, she puts some rather severe limits on his being out with friends. This provokes a defensive reaction from him, and he begins to see her as dictatorial, unloving, and nosey. They easily set each other off, and the situation gets progressively worse. Unfortunately, neither knows they are in the box because they are self-deceived as to why they are acting as they are.

One Friday night, he asks to use the car. She doesn't like it, so she puts an unreasonable time on him, telling him he has to be in by 10:30 p.m. After he leaves, she feels resentful and starts mentally blaming him again. Right at 10:30, she hears him drive up. But rather than being happy, she feels a keen pang of disappointment. What she needs most for all her blaming is for him to be blameworthy. Instead, he has come in on time. So, instead of praising his on-time arrival, she says, "You sure cut it close, didn't you?"

As this example illustrates, when another person acts like a jerk and we let ourselves get in the box, we'll <u>need</u> the other person to keep being a jerk so we can justify ourselves for blaming him. Our blaming keeps inviting the very behavior for which we blame them. In the box, we need problems.

All of us have probably done things like this. It happens a lot at work, as well as in the home. Over time, if the self-betrayal and the exaggerated blaming continue, these ways of thinking and acting become personality characteristics. We become fault-finders, needing to blame others to justify our self-deception. We also characteristically begin to treat people as objects, feeling that our own needs outweigh their own.

Another long-term effect is the distortion of our self-image, which begins to include many self-justifying images. We need to see ourselves as victims—horribly mistreated by others. People sense that in us and tend to live up to our expectations. As a result, we enter new situations already "in the box."

Many people go through life this way, never seeing the collusion because of their self-deception and their need to hold on to the exaggerated distortions. What they need most while in the box is to feel justified. So they blame others. And deep down, they really don't want the other person to quit being what they blame them for because they need to feel justified in their distortions.

When we are in the box, other people often live up to our negative expectations. Much that we do when we are in the box actually provokes other people to be what we are accusing them of being (or doing). But, we find that strangely "delicious" because it's proof that they are as blameworthy as we believed—and we're as much the innocent victim as we believed ourselves to be. The behavior that we complain about is the very behavior that justifies us. As a result, we unknowingly collude with each other to stay in the box.

When we're in the box, we focus on ourselves, often to the detriment of the co-workers or children in our program. If we see other people as objects rather than as real people, we provoke each other and then try to blame and control one other. Our reasons for blaming, however, are not to get someone to improve but to justify our own failure and self-deception. We look for faults because their shortcomings justify our failure to improve.

Even worse, this self-deception needs reinforcement. We feel a need to get others on our side. If we can convince them that we are victims of a horrible person, then we can continue to believe that someone else is to blame. In a work environment, however, this creates gossip, backbiting, lower commitment, troublemaking, stress, poor teamwork, lack of trust, and a host of communication problems. All of these problems come about as the result of self-betrayal. Organizations can be severely crippled by these problems.

It is important to remember that we get in the box because of self-betrayal-not because of the behavior of others (even if they are in their own box). Also, blaming does not help another person get out of the box. Blame serves only negative purposes, both for the individual and the organization.

An in-the-box leader can cause great problems within their organization. Other people will revert to their own boxes. Others will do what the boss insists only if the boss uses force or the threat of force. But that's not leadership. That's coercion. The boss will see fellow workers as lazy and uncooperative. They, in turn, will see her as dictatorial and pushy.

People in such situations need a way to get out of the box. Those who manage to do so find that it is liberating—not because they no longer have a need to demonstrate their virtue to others—but because the need to convince themselves will no longer be so overwhelming.

How do we get out of the box? First, let's describe what *doesn't* work. Trying to change a co-worker's behavior usually invites them to be defensive. "Coping" with them also doesn't work because it's just another way to continue blaming them. If they are in a box, it doesn't help them get out. Quitting a job doesn't generally help because we'll still be in the box. Neither does "communicating" between people in their boxes because we'll probably communicate blame. Even if we learn good interaction skills, it won't help much because we won't change our box-like feelings and misperceptions without it being just an attempt at manipulation. Praising others often fails because, in the box, we don't mean the positive things we say. Even trying to change our behavior in relation to the other person will have limited success because it keeps the focus on us.

Doing all of these things in the box will bring failure, or, at best, only limited success. To get out of the box, we need to stop the self-deception, the blaming, and regarding people as objects. This requires us to take an honest look at ourselves. We must stop betraying ourselves and be willing to question our own virtue. We must also question the exaggerated evil we see in others. We can ask ourselves if we are excusing ourselves from behaving in a kind way toward someone we have blamed for mistreating us. We need to honestly examine ourselves to ask if we have vilified or depersonalized an individual. To do this, we might ask ourselves if we engage in gossip with others, reveling in the misdeeds of this person. If so, we are very likely "in the box."

In will be easier to be honest with ourselves if we realize that life can be so much better out of the box than in it. Being a victim can make us feel vindicated, but it can also ruin our relationships and lead to chronic depression. Blaming others may let us off the hook for not doing what we know to be right, but it will cause us to fail to grow. In addition, it causes us to betray principles that could lift us to a higher plane in life. We cannot stop deceiving ourselves until we accept that we are doing so and realize that the harm we are doing to ourselves and those we love outweighs any potential benefits.

There are other things we must do in order to get out of the box. First, we should start seeing people as persons—not objects. This requires that we honor them as persons, with needs, hopes, and worries as real and legitimate as our own. It helps to think of them in roles we do not commonly associate with them (a boss, for example, is also a son or daughter, a friend, a father or mother, or a person who suffers just like we do). As we change our feeling for other persons, we can stop resisting them and start doing what their humanity calls for us to do. When we no longer need to blame others and inflate their faults, we can get out of the box.

The following suggestions are also helpful to those who truly want to get out of the box, especially in relation to their boss:

* Don't try to be perfect. Just try to be better.
* Don't use the expression "in the box" around people who don't know what it means. Use the principles quietly in your own life.
* Don't go around looking for (or pointing out) the boxes that others are in —keep a sharp eye out for your own.
* Don't give up on yourself when you realize you've slipped back into a box. Just keep trying.
* Admit you've been in a box when you have been. Apologize and keep moving forward, becoming ever more helpful.
* Change your focus from what others are doing wrong to what you can do right to help.

* Don't worry about whether others are helping you. Just be sure you are helping others.

Though we are not saying there are no bad bosses, this way of looking at relationships shifts the focus to something we can change- ourselves. In the words of the noted philosopher, Pogo, *"We have met the enemy, and **they is us**."*

Conclusion

Though we will not tell you that the principles of team leadership always work, they should help you deal with the vast majority of situations in dealing with your boss. In addition, you will increasingly enjoy the strength of unity that a team provides.

The principles and practices we have presented come at a critical time for early childhood educators. Each day, scientists discover more about the critical importance of a child's early years. So much depends on these children having teachers and programs that will be there for them and their parents. They deserve our best efforts.

Our best efforts result, however, not from us as individuals but as members of teams. Our resilience, our dedication, and our skills are closely linked to the support that team members give one another. As your team works together, being guided by fundamental principles and teaching each other sound practices, you will be successful. It is our hope that we have been helpful to you in this most noble endeavor.

Chapter Notes

1. Cited in Gene Bocialetti, *It Takes Two: Managing Yourself When Working with Bosses and Other Authority Figures* (San Francisco, Jossey-Bass Publishers, 1995) 147, 148.

2. Gene Boccialetti, *It Takes Two*, 165

3. Gene Boccialetti, *It Takes Two*, 165

4. Gary Namie and Ruth Namie, *The Bully at Work: What You Can Do to Stop the Hurt and Reclaim Your Dignity On the Job* (Naperville, Illinois: Sourcebooks, Inc., 2000) 270-272.

5. Carol Tavris and Carole Wade, *The Longest War: Sex Differences in Perspective* (New York: Harcourt, Brace, Jovanovich, 1984) 256-258.

6. *Ibid*, 255, 257.

7. Fast Company Magazine, edited by Anna Muoio, April 1999.

8. Stephen Covey, *How to Manage Your Boss*, http://interpersonal-skills.com

9. Norm Meshriy, Career Insights, 2001 at http://www. Career-insights. com/newpage13.htm

10. (San Francisco Business Times, July 16, 1999)

11. Gary and Ruth Namie, *The Bully at Work: What You Can Do to Stop the Hurt and Reclaim Your Dignity On the Job.* (Naperville, Illinois: Sourcebooks, Inc. 2000)

12. Stanley Bing, Crazy Bosses. (New York: Pocket Books, 1992) 129.

13. Suzette Elgin, *The Gentle Art of Verbal Self Defense* (Upper Saddle River, New Jersey, 2000)

14. Boccialetti, *It Takes Two*, 156.

15. Fred Luskin, *Forgive for Good: A Proven Prescription for Health and Happiness* (San Francisco: harper, 2001)

16. The Arbinger Institute, *Leadership and Self Deception: Getting Out of the Box* (San Francisco: Berrett-Hoehler Publishers, Inc. 2000)

Bibliography

Ackoff, Russell L. *Ackoff's Best: His Classic Writings on Management.* New York. John Wiley and Sons, Inc., 1999.

Arbinger Institute. *Leadership and Self Deception: Getting out of the Box.* San Francisco: Berrett-Hoehler Publishers, Inc., 2000.

Belasco, James A. and Ralph C. Stayer. *Flight of the Buffalo: Soaring to Excellence, Learning to Let Employees Lead.* New York: Warner Books, 1993.

Bing, Stanley. *Crazy Bosses: Spotting them, Serving Them, Surviving Them.* New York: Pocket Books, 1992.

Boccialetti, Gene. *It Takes Two: Managing Yourself When Working with Bosses and Other Authority Figures.* San Francisco: Jossey-Bass Publishers, 1995.

Briar-Lawson, Katharine. "The Rainmakers," (pp. 529-538) in Peter Senge (Ed.), *Schools that Learn.* New York. Doubleday, 2000.

Brilhart, J.K. "An Experimental Comparison of Three Techniques for Communication: A Problem-solving Pattern for Members of a Discussion Group," *Spech Monographs,* 33 (1966), Pp. 168-177.

Canfield, Jack and Mark Victor Hansen. *Chicken Soup for the Soul.* Dearfield Beach, Florida: Health Communications Incorporated, 1993

Covey, Stephen R. *Principle-Centered Leadership.* New York: Simon and Schuster, 1990.

Covey, Stephen. *How to Manage Your Boss.* http://interpersonalskills.com.

Dowd, Maureen. The *New York Times,* March 12, 1984, p. B1

Duncan, Roger Dean and Ed J. Pinnegar. *Leadership for Saints.* Covenant Communications, 2002.

Elgin, Suzette. *The Gentle Art of Verbal Self Defense.* Upper Saddle River, N.J.: Prentice Hall, 2000.

George, Jennifer M. and Gareth R. Jones. *Understanding and Managing Organizational Behavior.* Addison-Wesley Publishing Company: Reading Massachusetts, 1996.

Goleman, Daniel. *Working with Emotional Intelligence.* New York: Bantam Books, 1998.

Gouldner, Alvin. *Patterns of Industrial Bureaucracy.* New York: Free Press of Glencoe, 1954.

Hancock, LynNell and Pat Wingert. "The New Preschool," *Newsweek Special Issue: Your Child.* Spring/Summer, 1997.

Harvey, Jerry B. *The Abilene Paradox,* Lexington Books, 1988.

Henkoff, Ronald. "Finding, Training, and Keeping the Best Service Workers," in *Fortune,* October 3, 1994 (pp. 110, 114, 116).

Hummel, Ralph P. *The Bureaucratic Experience.* New York: St. Martin's Press, 1977.

Joyner, Edward T. "No More 'Drive-by Staff Development,'" (pp. 385-395) in Peter Senge (Ed.), *Schools that Learn.* New York. Doubleday, 2000.

Langford, David. (Starlink Conference). *Quality and Education: Critical Linkages.* October 12, 1993.

Lantieri, Linda. *Waging Peace in Our Schools.* Boston: Beacon Press, 1998.

Latane, Bibb, and John M. Darley. *The Unresponsive Bystander.* New York: Appleton, 1970.

Levine, James A. and Edward W. Pitt. *New Expectations: Community Strategies for Responsible Fatherhood.* New York: Families and Work Institute, 1995.

Lewin, Kurt. Group Decision and Social Change," in T. Newcomb and E. Hartley (Eds.), *Readings in Social Psychology.* New York: Holt, Rinehart and Winston, 1950.

Luskin, Fred. *Forgive for Good: A Proven Prescription for Health and Happiness.* San Francisco: Harper, 2001.

Maletz, Mark. *Fast Company Magazine.* April 1999.

Maslach, Christina and Michael P. Leiter. *The Truth about Burnout: How Organizations Cause Personal Stress and What to Do About It.* New York: Jossey-Bass, 1997.

Meshriy, Norm. "Career Insights, 2002," at http://www.Career-insights.com.

Milgram, Stanley. *Obedience to Authority.* New York: Harper, 1974.

Namie, Gary and Ruth Namie. *The Bully at Work: What You Can Do to Stop the Hurt and Reclaim Your Dignity on the Job.* Naperville, Illinois: Sourcebooks, Inc., 2000.

Negroni, Peter. "The Superintendent's Progress," (pp. 425-432) in Peter Senge (Ed.), *Schools that Learn.* New York. Doubleday, 2000.

Putnam, L.L., "Preference for procedural order in task-oriented small groups," *Communication Monographs*, 46, 1979. Pp. 193-218.

Romig, Dennis. *Breakthrough teamwork: outstanding results using structured teamwork.* Chicago: Irwin Professional Publishing, 1996.

Rosenthal, Robert, and Lenore Jacobsen. *Pygmalion in the Classroom.* New York: Holt, 1968.

Sands, Bill. Motivational talk to Lamar Community College, Lamar, Colorado. March 1970.

Tavris, Carol and Carole Wade. *The Longest War: Sex Differences in Perspective.* New York: Harcourt, Brace, Jovanovich.,1984.

Tavris, Carol. *Anger: The Misunderstood Emotion.* New York: Simon and Schuster, 1982.

Terkel, Studs. *Working: People Talk about What They Do All Day and How They Feel about It.* New York: The New Press, 1997.

Walton, Sam and John Huey. *Sam Walton: Made in America.* New York: Doubleday, 1992.

Whitla, Dean K. *Value Added: Measuring the Impact of Undergraduate Education.* Cambridge, Mass. Harvard University Press, 1965.

Whyte, William Foote. *Industry and Society.* New York: McGraw-Hill, 1946.

Index

Accountability, vi,7, 48, 102, 110, 137
Ackoff, Russell, 104, 117
Agenda, using for meetings, 15, 52, 71, 72, 93, 104
Anger, dangers and benefits of, 150-151
Arbinger Institute, 153, 159
Authority vs. coercion, 140-142, 157
Autocratic management, 5-9, 17, 25, 42
Bosses, difficult and bad, 135-142
Boss-style management, v, 16,17, 19, 23, 28, 31, 42, 47, 55, 98, 110
Boundaries, establishing between work and personal life, 119, 129, 130
Box, getting out of the, 153-158
Brainstorming, structured, 63, 64, 82, 136, 138, 141-152, 159
Bullying in the workplace, don't tolerate, 136, 138, 141, 146-152, 159
Bureaucracy, efficiency vs. effectiveness, 4, 8, 16,
Bureaucracy, problems with, 2-7, 19, 24, 127
Burnout, v, 124-130, 132
Carrot-and stick approach, v, 8, 16, 17
Cause, commitment to, v, 44, 78, 80, 96, 97, 125, 142, 144
Celebrations, importance of, 25, 45, 50, 72, 88, 144
Checking understanding, as a team skill, 70, 145
Coaching, 41, 42, 94, 99, 101, 102
Communication lines, as a structural variable, 42
Communications, establishing effective, 104-107
Competition, minimize among team members, 98, 148
Concept, use in outlining 106
Conflict resolution, 102, 107-110, 145, 146
Consensus, building, 1, 3, 65, 69, 70, 75, 89, 92, 109, 116
Control, external, 20